C

OCCASIONAL

For my mother

CRITIQUE PASSIONNÉE OR
A *FOLIE À TROIS* (2014)

These essays are all works of criticism concerned with the architectural present. Together they argue that it is now time to stop taking this contemporary present for granted, as if it were a natural affair, and to think it anew as a constructible space of action. Manufacturing a contemporary present requires a new mode of historical thinking, of course, but the more specific premise of this collection is that there can be no present in a general sense without an articulated theory of the contemporary for architecture in particular. Architecture has always seen itself – and been seen by others – as the home of the past and as the cultural form that best confers the status of history on the flotsam and jetsam of life. So to undo the attachment between architecture and certain forms of historical thinking is not only to dislodge architecture from unrecognised historicisms but also to open a present in the broadest possible terms. If even architecture – the proverbial medium of slowness, stillness and permanence – can be made to move lithely with the present, then contemporaneity in general may be possible.

The first section of this volume is made up of what I call *Occasional* essays, texts instigated by the appearance of architectural issues that are self-evidently current but also often mistakenly considered to be of minor concern or stature. For example, no one who looks upon the world today could fail to see the sheer range of colours on display or at least objects coloured in ways that differ significantly from the fantasy of an all-white modernist world. Nor could anyone who touches anything from a kitchen counter to a toothbrush fail to notice that plastic has given rise to a new family of forms and designed a new and increasingly comprehensive sensorium. Yet these and other novelties that appear to be natural attributes of the present are also de facto responses to traditional questions posed by the architectural discipline. Colour, to continue the example, is an aspect of the contemporary that must be considered at least in part through the way its perception has been shaped by the discipline's historical discourses. Thus, in the organisation of this book, topics such as plasticity or soft form function as concrete accrual suspended in a wide historical wash, the occasion for broad speculations on the narrow matter of contemporary form-making camouflaged as loose historical narratives.

The second set of texts, grouped under the term *temporary*, explores specific and short-lived events that took place during the 1960s, taken as the nascency period of today's present. The 1960s, I argue, is not in fact the decade that began in 1960, but rather the eruption of a socio-intellectual crease between history and the present. While the fold between then and now has a long and varied historical trajectory, as an object of study it is consistently the territory of the greatest intellectual and theoretical intensity – it is where the 'action' is, to use a phrase that itself dates from 1965. The individual essays in this second section are as narrowly focused as the essays in the first are expansive, and as archivally grounded as the others are survey-like. But they share with the *Occasional* essays a deliberate interest in minor and fleeting objects of study. Using discos and fashion boutiques – never before deemed worthy of scholarly investigation – these essays concoct historically exacting structures out of nothing, or what the field has deemed to be nothing. By systematically seeking events of apparently negligible consequence and reinforcing architectural acts as evanescent as a shag rug with the rigours of traditional scholarship, the *Temporary* section activates minor historical agents in order to prepare them to perform on the contemporary field. I do not argue that these tiny topics had an influence that has been overlooked, in the tradition of revisionist scholarship.

Rather, I intend for them to have an impact now that
they were unable to achieve then, in the tradition of what
Gilles Deleuze calls 'minor literature'. The second section,
then, comprises a series of manifestly historical essays that
together construct a genealogy for an alternative present.

The third group of essays reflects on this present,
or on the *contemporary* as actively constructed through
ideas of the ephemeral and provisional. In order to
deliberately obfuscate the difference between material that
is old, but made new through interpretation, and material
that is chronologically recent, but requires historicisation
to become contemporary, some things – for example
well-known works by Paul Rudolph (obviously old) and
lesser known works by Rudolph (old but seen by many
now for the first time) – are presented more than once in
different essays. All of these texts collect material that has
not properly entered the historical record, either because
it has seemed too embedded and obdurately self-evident
(like the colour which washes all over Rudolph drawings
but has been little noticed), or too fleeting, like colour
(which in many ways defined Rudolph interiors but today
is deliberately avoided in the scholarly literature). The
combined checklists construct a single if provisional
archive of what I call invisible form, work that has not
been hidden from view but that has nevertheless not been
historically witnessed.

Another important attribute shared by all the essays
in this volume is the ambition to bring writing into a closer
relationship with other dimensions of architectural design.

Writing and design were once quite intimate but
their gradual separation was an inevitable product of
modernity's calls for autonomy and specialisation. Not only
did the two part, but each dimension further fragmented
until the ultimate splitting of writing into distinct fields
called theory, history and criticism was finally institution-
alised. But in the era just before the professionalisation
of the architectural writer, in the era that gave rise to
the need for professional PhDs in architecture, figures like
Heinrich Wölfflin, Sigfried Giedion and Philip Johnson

wrote in close contact with design, deployed historical knowledge and theoretical concepts in various measures, and above all combined them to produce a form of criticism identifiable by the techniques of its prose, where extreme rhetoric goes beyond the actual phenomena being described, forcing often-disparate facts into an apparent coherence. Such coherences made it possible for modern architectural design and practice to survive in an increasingly inhospitable world and gave writing on architecture a tremendously broad significance – where would Deleuze or Umberto Eco be without Wölfflin?

Writing today is more professionally specialised than it was in the 1930s, but this hard-earned disciplinarity has made it almost impossible to conceive that it was precisely promiscuity and conviction that gave writing on architecture a cultural impact. Manfredo Tafuri, for example, considered the force exerted by the texts of the 1930s a form of historical brutality. His term, *critique passionnée*, did not merely describe the fervour of polemical language but was meant to expose the overdetermination of texts that were carried away by their passions. This invocation of emotion suggests it was less the committed nature of the writing that Tafuri opposed than a certain intimacy between writer and subject, and a language that betrayed writers moved by their subject and trying to move others in turn. Criticism after Tafuri came to denote writing that contained embarrassing outbursts of feeling that needed to be isolated from the supposedly scientific nature of architecture. Theory was the first means of stilling those unverifiable passions, and the best writing of the late 1970s to the early 1990s had this mission as one of its most energising purposes. More recently, as theory itself came to be associated with passions of its own, history stepped in to offer increasing expertise with diminishing affective force. Tafuri's belief that writing 'needs to keep its distance from … practice' and that the writer's 'proper task [is] objective and unprejudiced historical diagnosis' is no longer a critical correction but pseudo-scientific doxa.

Writing needs criticism and its associated promiscuities. The theoretical turn had a broader impact than the more recent historical turn, but passionate critics from Wölfflin to Reyner Banham, neither exclusively theorists nor historians, are a better model for criticism today. Transgressing the proper distance as they all did is the first element of a new definition of criticism as a medium specific to architectural writing because it will initiate a new romance between criticism and design by opening the space of fantasy and imagination, rather than over-idealisation, and therefore making production possible. Intimacy makes criticism an issue not of corroboration or corrigibility, but rather of position and participation. Its very passions are those which will put an end to the false-positivisms that still plague our field.

Criticism today must benefit from both history and theory but more importantly deploy the forms of argumentation that are born of the alchemy of an occasion, of a milieu, of social exchange. Such rootedness in the short duration of an event enables language to develop particularly keen ways of analysing phenomena and discerning fluctuations of the sensory world. *Knowing* rather than scientific, criticism designs the world with such vital conviction that it compels the world to reorganise itself around this image. Criticism uses its intimate knowledge of architecture to get excruciatingly close while remaining wary of the attractions of false facts. The result will be *critique passionnée*, ready to use its trespasses to add value to that architecture which it closely engages.

TEMPORARY

THE TEMPORARY CONTEMPORARY
(2002)

At some point during the 1950s, modern architecture
became contemporary. While this displacement began in
the 1940s and can be tracked through myriad forms, the
shift was complete by 1954. In that year, Sigfried Giedion
published *A Decade of Contemporary Architecture*, in which
he describes the 'consolidation of the whole movement'.
This publication reveals a distinct struggle with the
nomenclature of a phenomenon that Giedion argues began
in 1947, with titles shifting between 'new', 'recent', 'modern'
and so forth, settling down uneasily and with reservations
to *contemporary* in 1954.[1] That same year, the editors of
Architectural Record compiled *A Treasury of Contemporary
Houses*.[2] While all the featured houses were described as
modern, the editors also claimed that these houses resisted
and exceeded doctrinaire definitions of the modern:
'Why should a modern house have to have a flat roof?
Or a glass wall? Or an open kitchen? Why should it have to
have its structure exposed? Why shouldn't it have anything
its owners really want, including a curve or two, even a
Victorian curve?'

For the editors of the *Record*, the contemporaneity
of these houses lay in this excess desire. Unlike Giedion,
whose struggle to define the contemporary led him to
simply extend modern categories like structure, urbanism
and social improvement, they asserted the contemporary's
specifically anti-modern character: these modern houses
had become contemporary by acquiring nothing more
(but nothing less) than a 'new look'. Replacing the prewar
emphasis on firmness and commodity, they seized upon
the element of the Vitruvian triad that the modern

movement had neglected and argued that 'delight is the current fashion'.[3] When modern architecture became contemporary it shifted allegiance away from industrial production, the fortitude of engineering and an ethos of purification, forging new relationships with interior design, decoration, fashion and above all with the quixotic pleasures and designed obsolescence of consumer culture.[4] Despite the basic undertone of conflict in Giedion and of celebration in the editors of the *Record*, both efforts to periodise modernism did so by restricting prewar modernism to architectural fixations and dispersing postwar modernism into decorative supplements. In other words, in the logic of mid-century rhetoric, the modern house had, by 1954, come to be dressed up in a contemporary style.[5]

   This shift from modern architecture to contemporary style reflects a series of radical and complexly interwoven transformations. On the one hand, the shift describes a historical phenomenon, a specific condition that was triggered by the impact on the modern movement of social, economic and cultural developments occurring during and just following the Second World War. On the other hand, the shift was also the product of historical thinking (as demonstrated by Giedion, for example), because as modernity came to be historicised during those same years, the contemporary emerged as modernity's potential opposite – that which would betray modernity's limits – rather than its synonym. Similarly, the notion of style threatened to turn from a superficial attribute of architecture into a new cultural modality that would not only dominate cultural production as a whole but would test the limits of architecture in particular. In these epistemological terms, perhaps most importantly, the contemporary – as it emerged historically in 1954 – announced and articulated a speculative terrain and a sensibility that is not historically determined or temporally bound. Modernism *was* contemporary by 1954, but the contemporary *is* modern with fashion sense. Today, the difference between being modern and being contemporary relates to but exceeds the differences that existed at mid-century. The modern movement understood itself to constitute a fruition of a historical development, crowning the timefulness of classical eternity by substituting it with timelessness. *Tomorrow's House*, a 1945 compilation by George Nelson and Henry Wright of *Architectural Forum*, equivalent in many respects to *A Treasury of Contemporary Houses*, and often mistaken as a harbinger of postwar developments, actually enjoined the reader to be *modern*. Nelson and Wright promised that architecture could end the past by capturing the future: 'if one were to take the best planning ideas, the best structural schemes and the best equipment that have gone into the best modern houses, and combine them appropriately in a single house, the result would look like something out of the day after tomorrow'.[6] Nelson and Wright's injunctions against style ('you will find no catalogues of "styles" [here], no orations on good taste'), against fashion ('individuality in houses, as in people, is a fundamental expression of something real. It has nothing to do with fashion'), against specificities of all kinds ('the room with no name'), were efforts to shield modernity from anything that could betray temporal contingencies.[7] Tomorrow's House, they prophesied, would collapse architecture into a world of forever modern.

The contemporary, on the other hand, while shaped by the processes of modernisation, wanted to be with time. The contemporary was a style that announced itself as such by foregrounding its temporary features. Fashion became the logic to follow rather than the menace to avoid, and the key characteristic of fashion is change – to be of the moment is also to be inherently fleeting. And so the contemporary is necessarily constructed through temporary features: its decorative patterns, its collectibles, its very stylishness. Contemporary architecture of the 1950s was an architecture that integrated zones of intensity and delight into the cool and neutral spaces of modernism: the hot corner window of a postwar Neutra house gave to modernism a moment of contemporaneity.[8]

Contemporary architecture was not just the architecture of fashion in the 1950s in literal terms, and is not just all architecture at the moment it is built. The Salk Institute was never contemporary, not even in 1961, although it was certainly modern. On the other hand, Philip Johnson's Glass House – still used as the setting for fashion shoots – has perhaps only ever been contemporary. Contemporaneity is not, nor was it ever, a default; it is not synonymous with existing in or representing the present's essence and thus differs fundamentally from zeitgeist. Rather, to become contemporary is a project and an ambition that requires the identification of an architectural terrain that activates the sensibility of being with time and does so through a definable repertoire of operations. The most important manoeuvre of the contemporary, made apparent by the concept's affiliation with fashion, was to reject modernity's reliance on the notion of an ideal state. The second effect sought by the contemporary, equally born of modernity's conviction that time could be actively shaped, was to resist arresting or transcending time and instead push time itself towards a dynamic/fluid state.

Through this newly fluid temporality, the contemporary makes available a neglected dimension of architecture itself. Not so much a quality of architecture as a function, it begins where architecture is supposed to end but does not, encompassing the treatment of lighting, of decoration, of objects, of surface, of geometry, of beauty, of 'delight'. If modernism inhibited such effects and architecture historically identifies them as supplemental, a contemporary practice stages itself as such through activating the effects that architecture inevitably produces but rarely confirms. The contemporary is an architectural strategy that expands the internal logic of the discipline by identifying as 'architectural' phenomena generally located outside the discipline.

To reconsider architecture in relation to the sensibility of the contemporary requires analytical tools unencumbered by the traditional identification between the 'sachlichkeit' of the modern movement and the techniques and supposed objective neutrality of the modern architectural historian. Theorising the contemporary requires instead tools able to admit architecture's mobilisation of temporary effects, a territory recognised neither by the modern movement itself nor by its master narrators. However, just as contemporaneity was produced yet unclaimed by modern architecture, its description and analysis requires a historical methodology that also was produced yet unclaimed by the modern movement's historians. They too sought to foreground as rational and self-evident ideas such as the dominant role of technology in the shaping of modern architecture or the inevitability of the triumph of function over form. Yet in their very effort to convince their readers they also relied on powerfully tendentious rhetorical strategies making their texts more potent in their effects than necessarily compelling through their facts. Today we can historicise and thereby produce the contemporary by relying on argument to make facts persuade a possible present into being rather than by organising history into a shapely narrative. The historian of the contemporary operates, then, as a scavenger, picking and choosing from a past conceived as an annal – a disparate collection of events and effects – rather than as an archive – a coherent arrangement of causes. This approach to curating history by putting things into provisional relation with one another, like the strategies of architecture in the contemporary, seeks to achieve a potent yet fleeting mise-en-scène.

Sir John Soane, who not only repeatedly rearranged his own milieu but has himself repeatedly been rearranged by historians, is a useful cipher for thinking the contemporary. Lincoln's Inn Fields is simultaneously a home and a museum; or rather it is a structure that houses both domesticity and museology.[9] Soane spent much of his life assembling his collection of antiquities, paintings, models, mirrors and so forth, as well as amassing the collection of buildings that houses these objects. The collapsed distinction between dwelling and collecting continues today with the sense of ownership and intimacy conveyed by the curators of the John Soane House and Museum – they seem as much like inhabitants as they do caretakers. Recent scholarship has similarly focused on the difference between public and private spheres within the Soane House, as well as on its relationship to collecting and representation.[10] In fact, Soane has been recreated by almost every architectural generation of the twentieth century. His work has been used to establish a patrimony for the elimination of ornament from architecture, for abstraction, for historicist post-modernism, for spectacularity. The constant reinvention of Soane is not accidental, but rather is evidence of how the house mobilises the mood of contemporaneity. As the collections grew and sought their final staging, the house had to be continually updated and revised. The architecture was generated by an impulsive fluidity that opens the house to temporality and permits it to be reinstalled with every new contemporary imaginary. Soane was a pack rat – he was not just a collector, but a

Joseph Gandy,
Watercolour view of Sir
John Soane's Museum, 1811

compulsive, with excessive multiples in each category of his collection. The collection is not precisely encyclopedic, but repetitive. It did not produce a comprehensive assemblage of unique objects within a class – every different kind of capital, for example. His library was filled with several copies of the same book, just as the breakfast room is articulated with many of the same kind of mirror.[11] The story of the house is, in part, the story of finding the proper place for this improper quantity of things. As Soane acquired more and more possessions he needed more and more buildings to house them: not just for storage, but for display. As the collections became permanent, the architecture became temporary, afflicted by an almost relentless rebuilding and restaging.

The shape of the house is a result of the collections, and in turn was called upon to showcase them with maximal effect. Soane developed an elaborate bag of tricks to add a range of characters and moods to his collection. Perhaps the most dramatic of his techniques – in addition to his experiments with lighting, sectional complexity and optical devices – was the treatment of the wall, or rather of its surface. Laminated at moments, as in the Picture Room, encrusted at others, as in the Dome, the surface itself became a special effect. Treated in utterly inconsistent ways through the house, it never creates a predictable system. It is in that sense that Soane's surfaces are concerned with effect: they have no legible cause. While they are effective insofar as they de-emphasise causality and legibility, the surfaces also accentuate and dramatise their effectiveness. At this moment of heightened purpose the surfaces generate not merely effects, but *special* effects. And special effects, unlike ordinary effects, risk becoming obsolete, yet in that risk of becoming lies their contemporaneity.

If Soane's museum was also a house, most of Mies van der Rohe's houses were also museums. The Resor House (1937–39) was largely organised around works of art, and has been specifically related to Mies's later work on museums.[12] More importantly, the Miesian house frames and produces museological vision: everything within these houses, from garbage to furniture, is subject to the attention of the museum-goer and thus absorbed into the logic of the museum, a museum dedicated to showing a permanent collection. The conflict between Mies and Edith Farnsworth can be framed as being about who would curate the exhibition space generated by the house,[13] but it was also a conflict over the temporalities of the exhibition itself. In the end, Mies installed the house by staging a permanent showing of domesticity in which nothing temporary was permitted. This museological entombing of time is similarly manifest in the gaze solicited by the Resor House and its collage. Pasted onto the window, the landscape painting is endlessly on view. The landscape does not change, the view does not change, the gaze does not change. The house creates an eternal present by framing time as realised in a single display.

The optical collapse of the museum house into the eternity of the modern was reinforced by Mies's interest in the single-space pavilion and the large-span building.[14] In opening architecture to a discussion of effects without reliance on phenomenology or essentialism – there has been no evoking of the essence of materials or the phenomenon of vision here – Mies must be considered a master. His interest in the effects of surfaces and in their collective coordination is the feature of his work that generates the most intense accumulation of modern atmosphere.[15] Moreover, this particular means of curating a modernist mood is what most radically distinguishes Mies from Le Corbusier, who always remained less interested in the effects of surface than in its legibility. By the same token, Mies's mood was always modern, not contemporary.

In contrast to Soane's special effects, Mies was interested in all-over effects, the uniformity of which was best underscored by the single-space pavilion. In these pavilions, there is little differentiation from zone to zone as all is absorbed into a continuous set of conditions. That is not to say that the phenomenon of the house is not subject to change – the sun does shine in varying degrees on the Farnsworth House – but the effects aspire to constancy. Similarly, the Photoshop quality of the Resor collage allows no real foreground or background and creates instead spatial evenness and topological equivalence. In other words, while there are Miesian effects, there are no Miesian *special* effects. The manifold uniformity of his palette of effects was the means for Mies to stage modernist time. Lacking special effects, the Farnsworth House is not contemporary. It was modern when it was new, remains modern today and will always be modern.[16]

While the Farnsworth House is often cited as the point of departure for the first version of the Eames House, the Eameses are better understood as the spiritual heirs of Soane, with a twist. Perhaps less compulsive as collectors than he, they were undoubtedly more obsessive as curators: domesticity for the Eameses consisted largely in rearranging their possessions, [17] of which, like Soane, they had massive quantities. But unlike Soane, whose house changed radically over time to accommodate his collections, the Eames House remained more or less constant while the installation of interiority was in a continuous state of reorganisation. Their notions of 'functioning decoration' and 'object overload' are perhaps more important as keys to their curatorial strategies than as justifications for their excessive collecting. Their house was a stage for an ever-changing series of exhibitions of an ever-increasing range of domestic miscellany that grew in scale and density until it not only became a field through which the architectural surface was necessarily seen but ultimately subsumed the architectural surface itself into the display's provisional and temporary logic.

Every surface of the Eames House was partially covered by another surface: blankets on sofas, rugs on the floor, paintings suspended from the ceiling. Each of these partial surfaces was further kaleidoscoped by an excessive number of edges and frames – the large windows maximised rather than minimised the possible number of frames and mullions; why have only one square edge of a rug when three will do better; and so forth. Over time, the surfaces had less and less to do with the division of space or the articulation of structure, and more to do with the proliferation of display opportunities. The interior became a topology of exposition, soliciting a continuous reconsideration of the curatorial impulse and producing spectacular effects. If Mies framed a permanent view, the Eameses multiplied the frame to produce not a view but an atmosphere of contemporary viewing. Like the relentless jump cuts of an MTV video, the agitation of the surfaces made the house into an enormous special effect.

The most significant technique used in the production of the Eames House atmosphere and 'look' is the super-ficiality of the surface. Although surfaces accumulate, they are conceived and exposed as thin picture planes: in their later work and in their work on actual exhibitions the Eameses' ideal surface component became the moving

filmic image without material depth of any kind. Peter
and Alison Smithson, on the other hand, thickened the
architectural surface, using its viscous porosity to stage a
new array of temporal effects, and using the categories
of consumer culture to this end. The House of the Future
(1956–57), with its highly stylised mannequins, showroom
atmosphere and hip look, fully embraces the delights
and evanescence of the postwar fashion house. In fact the
house, along with related projects such as the Appliance
House, theorises a new range of architectural durations.

The Smithsons explicitly reframed modernism's
approach to the installation of domestic objects and the
treatment of surfaces as opportunities for display in
relation to different modes of measuring time. The House
of the Future, for example, engorged appliances. Rather
than leaving them exposed – as Le Corbusier's sink at the
Villa Savoye stood isolated, worshipped as an enduring
monument to the future – the Smithsons absorbed
refrigerators, vacuums and televisions into malleable walls.
The kinds of consumables that gave shape and dimension
to the architecture were specifically durable, and therefore
temporal, goods. The car to which they likened the
Appliance House was not the timeless, standard-seeking
automobile of Le Corbusier, but a temporary ideal that was
subject to annual change. As they wrote, 'The Appliance
House gives the appliances definite areas in which to
operate, … defining the space, whilst the inside can be
stripped-out and re-equipped when the owner's or fashion's
changing needs and methods demand.' [18] The plasticity
of the surface permitted durable goods to become poché,
making whatever remained of the idea of permanence
itself vestigial. Finally, if the thickened surfaces of the
walls permitted the house to consume durable consumer
goods, they also gave additional display space to objects
of shorter aesthetic duration. Extreme fashion became
the primary means of articulating the interior's visual
field. The inhabitant of the House of the Future is literally
being fashioned, in the process of being styled, getting
'glamorous' and contemporary.[19] This newly emerging

contemporary subject, in other words, both like her
surroundings and because of her surroundings, was
specifically fashioned to understand herself as always
under formation. Unlike the modernist subject, who
was generally rendered homogeneous in the effort to
secure ideal form and protection from the vulgarities
of commercial culture, the contemporary subject made
unprecedented forms of difference possible. In fact, this
new form of differentiated subjectivity in the contemporary
was only possible within the unfixed and constantly
shifting terrain of consumption.

By the 1960s, the furniture showroom had become the
site of the most advanced ideas of architectural contemporaneity. If architecture had once been called on to curate the
contemporary through its installation of effective objects,
architecture came to be challenged by that which it had
once taken care of in a kind of Oedipal play. Verner Panton's
Visiona II environment for the Cologne Furniture Fair of
1970, or Joe Colombo's Visiona 69, allow one to understand
domesticity through the field of effects deployed by the
temporary installation of decorative objects. These projects
eliminate traditional notions of modern architecture,
lacking above all else the ethical mandate of modernism:
they have no depth, no moral, no rectitude. Instead, they
have intense fashion sense. Such projects demonstrate the
importance of presenting the surface as manifestly effective
rather than tectonic when architecture seeks mood instead
of meaning. Here, topologies of continuous colour, texture
and animation eliminate any traditional 'frame' of vision
and thus provide no mechanism to ensure that the viewer
gazes at a particular object. Without the concentrated gaze
of the museum-goer, the objects have no source of temporal
stability and provide none to the environment.

Since the nineteenth century, historians have
considered the relationship between the human subject
and the architectural object and as different as theories
of empathy, for example, might be from phenomenology,
they tend to share the view that objects have effects
and act on subjects. In contrast, the contemporary opens

up the possibility that the reverse is a more interesting proposition, and that architectural objects should be conceived instead as upheld and held together by subjects. In this view, the temporal stability of modernism was the effect of the steady gaze of a stable subject while the fluctuating temporalities of the contemporary are the effect of multiple subjects in formation. The contemporary subject not only exercises agency through the logic of effects but this agency increases as effects grow in variety and number. Finally, this dynamic whereby the architectural object is produced in and through the subject differentiates the contemporary from pure spectacle, which is typically understood as overwhelming and arresting the subject.

The contemporary beholder actively seeks out a superabundance of special visual effects in order to produce a kind of diversionary vision: not the distraction of the everyday, or the mundane or the banal, but a visual mode that is at once diffuse and oversaturated. These conditions have been observed before and have generally been described in terms of how they dematerialise architecture. A good example would be the standard interpretations of Bernard Tschumi's Video Gallery built in Groningen in 1990. Rather than accept the intellectual *léger de main* that is required in order to argue that, in this case, glass and light are not materials and can cause dematerialisation, they should be understood as symptoms of the reorientation of architecture towards a field of effects. As Tschumi operated on the glass box, the house lost its modern building and turned into an effectively programme-free zone of special effects. At this moment of spectacularisation, the gallery gained its capacity to have the 'look' of contemporary architecture.

This is not a mysterious, indefinable or purely phenomenological condition. In fact, the projects described herein constitute a measurable and even qualifiable body of research concerned with a particular set of issues and generating an identifiable palette of techniques. Of paramount importance has been the de-emphasising of volume, logic of plan and ethics of rationalism in favour of atmospheres produced through the curation of the surface. Through accumulation, lamination, decoration, colouration, agitation, plastification and environmentalisation, these surfaces curated effective moods, and when the effects were special, catalysed the contemporary. In fact, it is only through theorising the effect that the mysteries of the zeitgeist can give way to a substantive understanding of the contemporaneity and the shared sensibility of, say, Preston Scott Cohen's Torus House, Herzog & de Meuron's Ricola Headquarters *and* Soane's House. Despite distinct vocabularies and disparate historical moments, these projects marshal curatorial techniques in unapologetic investigations into surface effects.

Given these strategies, an effect may be understood as a condition that is detachable from the logic of causality. The greater the distance between the cause and effect, the greater the sense of effectiveness. The most common technique of producing this distance is distracted vision, a condition in which the visual field resists becoming a screen of legibility by making it impossible for attention to become concentrated and absorbed.[20] Thus, for example, modernist transparency appears as directly and causally linked to the material properties of glass: the modern movement made glass into a magic writing tablet that rationalised its effects. Contemporary luminescence, on the other hand, is an effect whose cause is not immediately visible, and is one that would be dissipated by enhanced legibility. Effects are dissembling, provisionary and contemporary. Special effects are especially conditional and experimental – like an avocado kitchen counter or a Replicant, they sense their impending demise. But in incorporating an expiration date, their shelf life, however short, can be especially vivid. *The Matrix* had the hot look of today until it became banal and everyday. Special effects thus curate contemporaneity itself, and while the architecture of special effects yields to modernity a place in eternity, it claims for itself the moment of now.

First published in *Perspecta* 34 (2003)

NOTES

1. Sigfried Giedion first published
   A Decade of New Architecture in
   1951. The second edition, published
   three years later, has two title
   pages, both set in three languages:
   French and German titles remain
   consistent: 'Dix ans d'Architecture
   Contemporaine' and 'Ein Jahrzehnt
   moderner Architektur'. The English
   title appears as 'A Decade of New
   Architecture' in a small point size on
   the first title page and as 'A Decade
   of Contemporary Architecture' in
   a large point size on the second title
   page. The second edition contains
   an appendix on the years 1947–54,
   which Giedion, in his preface to
   the second edition, describes as
   a 'supplemental covering' of the
   'further consolidation of the whole
   architectural movement'.

2. *A Treasury of Contemporary
   Houses Selected by the Editors
   of Architectural Record*
   (New York, NY: FW Dodge, 1954).

3. Emerson Goble, 'Introduction'
   to *A Treasury of Contemporary
   Houses*, op cit, v.

4. Still today, common associations
   with postwar contemporary design
   'are heightened expressiveness,
   broader ranges of colour and shape,
   and a mood of pleasure rather
   than austerity'. See Lesley Jackson,
   *Contemporary: Architecture
   and Interiors of the 1950s* (London:
   Phaidon, 1994).

5. Another way to articulate the
   same historiographical point,
   which constitutes something of
   a digression in this context, would
   be that as postwar architecture
   dispersed into contemporaneity
   and into architecture's decorative
   supplements, it produced a
   consolidated view of prewar architecture characterised by strictly
   architectural fixations. Despite
   the differences in the manifest
   attitude toward the contemporary
   of the texts by Giedion and the
   editors of *Record*, both efforts
   to delimit or at least define the
   contemporary brought into being
   the very modernity with which
   the contemporary was contrasted.
   In other words, it can be said
   more precisely that the modern
   house was laid bare only when
   by 1954 it came to be dressed up
   in a contemporary style.

6. George Nelson and Henry Wright,
   *Tomorrow's House: How to plan
   your postwar home now* (New York,
   NY: Simon and Schuster, 1945), 8.
   This book is often interpreted
   as a harbinger of the distinctiveness
   of postwar architecture. My
   argument, however, is that while
   the book may contain material
   often periodised as 'postwar',
   its theoretical concerns remain
   entirely modern and indeed helped
   constitute the very modernity
   with which it is contrasted.

7. Ibid., 9, 7, 76–80.

8. On the corner in Neutra, see
   Sylvia Lavin, 'Richard Neutra
   and the Psychology of the
   American Spectator', *Grey Room*,
   Fall 2000, 42–64.

9. The basic Soane literature includes
   D Stroud, *Sir John Soane, architect*
   (London: Faber & Faber, 1984)
   and P de la Ruffinière du Prey,
   *John Soane, The Making of An
   Architect* (Chicago, Il: University
   of Chicago Press, 1982).

10. On this aspect of Soane, see
    Helene Furjan, 'The Specular
    Spectacle of the House of
    the Collector', *Assemblage* 34
    (December 1997), 57–92.

11. For a brief discussion of this aspect
    of Soane's library, see Sylvia Lavin,
    *Quatremère de Quincy and the
    Invention of a Modern Language*

of Architecture (Cambridge, MA: MIT Press, 1992), 177–81.

12. On the Resor House, both as a container for an art collection and in relation to the culture of collecting, see Cammie McAtee, 'Alien #5044325: Mies's First Trip to America', in P Lambert (ed), *Mies in America* (Montreal: Canadian Centre for Architecture, 2001), 132–91. Myron Goldsmith said of Mies in an interview in 1996, 'he was very interested in a container, whether it was glass or partly glass, a very simple container for all kinds of things. I think that that was in full swing about the time of the 50 x 50 House and beyond to the end of his life, Bacardí and the Berlin Museum and the other museum'. Cited by Lambert in *Mies in America*, 454.

13. Alice Friedman, 'Domestic Differences: Edith Farnsworth, Mies van der Rohe, and the Gendered Body', in Christopher Reed (ed), *Not At Home* (London: Thames and Hudson, 1996) 179–92; and Alice T Friedman, 'People Who Live in Glass Houses: Edith Farnsworth, Ludwig Mies van der Rohe, and Philip Johnson', in *Women and the Making of the Modern House, A Social and Architectural History*, (New York, NY: Abrams, 1998), 126–59.

14. On the single-span building, see Lambert, *Mies in America*, 423.

15. Some of the vast literature on Mies to focus on this aspect of his work includes Robin Evans, 'Mies van der Rohe's Paradoxical Symmetries' in *Translations from Drawing to Building and Other Essays* (London: AA Publications, 1997), 233–77; and Rosalind Krauss, 'The Grid, the Cloud and the Detail', in Detlef Mertins (ed), *The Presence of Mies* (New York, NY: Princeton Architectural Press, 1994), 133–48.

16. Recently, Mies has acquired some contemporaneity through the operations of Toyo Ito, Rem Koolhaas and others, allowing one to distinguish between otherwise apparently similar interests in modernism today. Unlike contemporary architecture, today's neo-modernism is simply current and mundane. In its disdain for special effects and the temporality of the provisional and experimental, neo-modern pragmatism cannot generate a contemporary project.

17. See the chapter on 'Functioning Decoration' in Pat Kirkham, *Charles and Ray Eames: Designers of the Twentieth Century* (Cambridge, MA: MIT Press, 1995).

18. Alison Smithson, 'The Future of Furniture', *Architectural Design (AD)*, April 1958, 178.

19. One criterion that the Smithsons included in their 'self-imposed programme' for the Appliance House was that it 'contain a glamour factor'. See Alison and Peter Smithson, 'The Appliance House', *AD* April 1958, 177.

20. On distracted and absorbed vision, see Walter Benjamin, 'The Work of Art in the Age of Mechanical Reproduction', in H Arendt (ed), *Illuminations* (New York, NY: Houghton, Mifflin, Harcourt, 1986), 217–52; Michael Fried, *Absorption and Theatricality: Painting and Beholder in the Age of Diderot* (Berkeley, CA: University of California Press, 1980) and Jeffrey Kipnis, 'The Cunning of Cosmetics', *El Croquis* 84 (1997), 22–29.

PLASTICITY AT WORK (2002)

Vilified by plastiphobes and touted as a panacea by plastiphiles, plastic is virtually everywhere. We are all always in some form of intimate contact with the stuff. It might be in your cavity-prone teeth, in your reconstructed knee, in your pre-saline breast implants and in the diet chips you ate for lunch. If it's not actually in your body, it's undoubtedly in your clothes, on the upholstery of your chair, in the paint on your walls and the mechanical systems of your building. And yet these examples notwithstanding, the one place plastic does *not* appear is in the disciplinary discourses of architecture. Even though one can barely think modern architecture without thinking materials – the glass house, the brick villa, the steel frame, the concrete city – there is no equivalent plastic typology. Plastic never earned a place in what Baudrillard called the aristocracy of materials; it lacks the essential and immutable qualities that authorised this supposedly natural hierarchy.[1] If glass was the modernist material par excellence, identified with utopia, truth and lightness, plastic was marked as a product of waste, commodification and masquerade. Unable to enter the moral logic based on an identity between materials and truth – truth to materials, truth of materials and so forth – plastic has remained an unethical unmentionable.

The problem may lie in plastic's very ubiquity. By the early 1970s, plastic – shiny, furry, puffy, squishy plastic – was taking over the domestic landscape, enveloping everything in its way. The range of colours made possible by the susceptibility of plastic to various forms of pigmentation grew; the palette of textures plastic could assume proliferated; the panoply of material effects plastics could mimic became virtually infinite. Plastic was everywhere, but in so many different forms that it could claim no stable identity. The plasticisation of the visual environment and of material life itself coincides with and in fact worked alongside a semiotic logic that was also taking over the cultural landscape during the same years. Objects, images and words, of whatever class, genre, medium and material, were being converted into signs, each with equivalent status and functionality in the chain of signification. Just as plastic molecules had no shape unless moulded by an external form, none of these signs were understood to possess stable meaning except that produced by differentiation from other signs. All things turned into plastic and into signs at the same time, forming in the process a logic of the plasticity of signs. In other words, plastics became both a material and a cultural sign. By orchestrating the convergence between the facets of plastic's double identity the period actively turned plastic into a super-signifier.

A pivotal episode in this drama of plastic playing between signifier (material without content) and signified (meaning without content) is the most famous cliché of them all, as uttered to Dustin Hoffman's character, Benjamin, in the 1967 film *The Graduate*: 'I want to say one word to you. Just one word: "Plastics"...' The single word both recalls the history of plastic's heroic rise into a material of utopia and proleptically announces the false idol's immanent collapse into semiotic dystopia. With exquisite economy the statement expresses the primal power attached to the notion of materiality as such as well as the duplicity of an endlessly malleable signifier able to take on the impressions and desires of any given moment and able to turn all things into signifiers. But the fact that this word, which once contained not one but two radical sets of assumptions, has now become a quip and worse, a cliché, constitutes an urgent call to think plastic beyond either of these regimes. Perhaps when plastic moved into the chain of signification, prodded as it was by architecture to do so, it was not as positively, passively and permanently integrated into the semiosphere as Roland Barthes and others argued.[2] Some trace of plastic might have been left on the plane of experience, a plane that by now should include both questions of matter and questions of sense. In which case, the real question becomes whether or not the peculiar double history of history can today be asked to yield something singular.

The absence of plastic as sign from architecture is ironic because historically the discipline has always been marked by plasticity, both in relation to its internal configuration (what architecture was understood to be made of, its literal and phenomenal material) and its outward effects (what and how architecture was to signify). No other of the visual arts has had its nature so radically and constantly redefined: sometimes architecture has been said to be about space. Other times, for millennia in fact, architecture knew of no such concept. During certain periods architecture's purpose was to organise purposefulness, while at others the effects of architecture were to be measured precisely in terms of surplus and excess. Perhaps because modernity is also itself an inconsistent phenomenon, riddled by moments of oscillation, the twentieth century opened architecture to the widest array of spaces of experimentation that demanded extraordinary agility. In so doing, modernity set architecture on a path towards ever stronger identification with its various forms of plasticity.

This trajectory is at another moment of intensity. People are abuzz about plastics today, just as they were in the 1960s and for the same two sets of reasons: because technical advances in material sciences have once again radically expanded the performance envelope of plastics and because the way we understand the relation of matter to culture, in other words how we conceive of materials as signifying, is also in a state of flux. But in the 1960s, even if plastic was described as infinitely supple, its very amenability was met with at least some degree of suspicion. Today, architecture is for the most part resolutely enjoying surfing the crest of this new neo-plasticism. A few have responded to this moment of historical plasticity with retrenchment, but far more seem to see in plastic's transformability a confirming parallel with architecture's own condition of perpetual malleability. Yet this is not the 1960s and it would be anachronistic to try to repeat that period's almost perfect formulation of plastic as super signifier. Instead, it is important to recognise the possibility that plastics, precisely as super signifier, have already been drained of theoretical potential by the field, and that the current easy absorption of plastics suggests less resonance with theories of signs (or theories about anything at all) and more the discipline's increasing tendency towards compliance. Material suppleness is a poor cover for professional acquiescence, and the best way to avoid such a category mistake is to mobilise architecture's historic plasticity and its historical discourses on plastics, however limited they may be, to generate from this material and intellectual genealogy a new rather than a repeated opportunity.

When Reyner Banham fell for Roger Vadim's *Barbarella* in 1968, he became more or less the first and only architecture critic to say anything interesting about the material. In his 1968 essay, 'Triumph of Software', Banham claimed that traditional architecture was giving way to a new form of responsive environment characterised by ambience and by curved, pliable, continuous, breathing, adaptable surfaces.[3] For Banham the success of Barbarella's world derived from the fact that it performed like flesh produced through natural materials such as fur and moss or their artificial equivalent: inflated, transparent plastic membranes. But Banham's opposition between hardware and software, between the traditional city of modernism and the plastic environment of the future, too easily saw plastic simply as a new technological means for furthering modernist ends. In contrast, precisely because of its lack of ethical and formal restrictions, plastic uncovers the material unconscious of a neglected modernity that resists the ideology of high modernism by occupying a position somewhere between culture and matter. *Barbarella*'s plastic artificial world is not opposed to the nature that authorised the Renaissance vision with which it has been compared, but stealthily just assumes its place: the ocean from which Venus emerges becomes, in *Barbarella*, the erotic plastic landscape of the chamber of dreams. Ultimately, this substitution deforms modernism's idealised representations. When Fonda is entrapped by gravity she is oddly disfigured by the perfect transparency of her plastic bed. In fact, it is modernity itself that is disfigured by a plastic already embedded within modernity's ideology.

There are certain irreducible aspects of plastic as a category of material that are incommensurable with the logic of modernism: plastic is a synthetic liquid material in a state of arrest. The combination of artificiality and instability defies the essentialising and naturalising of materials that were central to modernist discourse. If brick had such an unchanging and reliable nature that it could consistently tell you what it wanted to be, plastic does not adhere to any such universal grammar or authorise a material discipline. Material specificity and its role in modernist theories of architecture must be understood as paralleling discourses on the more general notion of medium specificity. Material identity was the primary means by which architecture sought to enter the logic of medium specificity, particularly around the mid-twentieth century, even though architecture had by then accumulated many forms of identity: function, structure and space, to name just a few. All these criteria were used to define architecture, yet none offered the clarity of definition that Clement Greenberg could offer to painting. In this context, truth to materials came to dominate because it offered the best means of overcoming architecture's plastic and shifting relation to medium. It was this fabricated link between medium and material specificity that plastic's arrival into the discourse in the 1960s unravelled because it revealed both forms of specificity to be constructed precisely via fiction and language.

Despite the many efforts to conflate them either through the fictions of science or the science of signs, plasticity as an ideology and an adjective can be

distinguished from plastic as a material and a noun.
The actual invention of plastics in the molecular sense
took place only during the nineteenth century. The ideological role of plasticity in the arts, however, is as old as
architectural discourse itself, and begins with Vitruvius.
His *Ten Books* are the first to have codified the 'plastic' arts,
one of many terms he took from the Greek, in this case
from *plassein*, meaning to mould. Vitruvius defined the
plastic arts in relation to the moulding process required
for their production: ceramics, stucco and plasters, even
sculpture, were characterised by their plasticity. This
rootedness in material and manual labour is what made
the plastic arts also the lesser arts. In contrast, Vitruvius
defined the liberal arts in relation to abstract rather than
formal or material properties. The liberal arts originated
not in a process of manufacture but in ideas produced
in the mind of the artist and thus were accorded a much
higher cultural status. Most importantly, the liberal arts
were those that signified via imitation, narrative and so
forth, while the plastic arts were those that were made in a
particularly fluid way. Thus, by the turn of the twentieth
century, when Le Corbusier defined architecture as a plastic
thing, *une chose de plastique* – a pure creation of the mind
that called not for the architect but for *le plasticien* – he was
referring to an antique ideology of form-making rather
than to a synthetic polymer or a vanguard rhetoric of
modern industrial materials.[4]

Although this fact has never been noted, almost
every major modern architect from Frank Lloyd Wright
to Le Corbusier, from Hannes Meyer to Richard Neutra,
was interested in this kind of plasticity and claimed it
as a defining and privileged feature of modernism. To take
just one example, Wright's famous essay, 'In the Nature
of Materials', was written in 1943, long before plastic had
become a significant factor in building construction: his
own primary contact with plastic was in the form of silicon
used in building with glass. Nevertheless, his essay claims
that plastic 'is peculiarly modern' and that 'plasticity' is
nothing less than 'the true aesthetic of genuine structural

reality'.[5] Unlike glass and steel, to which Wright assigns essential characteristics, plastic is a material without a nature, but plasticity is a concept with an aesthetic. Hence plastic both structures modernity and exceeds modernity's logic when taking the form of a material without an ethical mandate. Plastic has thus troubled the Vitruvian classification of the arts, by suggesting that architecture could both be plastic, defined in relation to its mode of production, and characterised by plasticity in relation to its mode of signification. Occupying the very space of this contradiction between the will to signify and the will to be formed, architecture has always been especially haunted by this disciplinary plasticity.

And never more so than during the 1960s, when the idea of plasticity complexly converged with an intense interest in the new materials of plastics. It was at this moment that plastic did its most energetic work in undoing modernism's authority and began to exploit the flexible structure of architecture's disciplinary instability. Three projects of the era can be used to explore this phenomenon: Claes Oldenburg's *Bedroom Ensemble* of 1963–69, Michael Webb's Cushicle of 1966–67 and Joe Colombo's Total Furnishing Unit of 1969–72. Each uses plastic in formally different ways: Oldenburg as a kind of industrial canvas, Webb as a skin and Colombo as a semi-solid block. All were considered prototypes primarily for exhibition purposes and all share a domestic programme. They are relatively minor projects, a choice necessitated by the fact that plastic has been excluded not only from the nobility of materials but from the nobility of the canon (it is still hard today to conceive of an architectural monument made of plastic). While differing significantly in cultural context and their configuration of domesticity, in formal character and their deployment of plastic, these works all use techniques of plasticity to interpose gaps into modern orthodoxies.

Oldenburg's *Bedroom Ensemble* was installed in the front room of the Sidney Janis Gallery in New York in 1964 for an exhibition titled 'Four Environments'.[6] Conceived while Oldenburg was living in Los Angeles and experimenting extensively with techniques of using plastic, from vacuum-forming to inflatables, the project evokes Oldenburg's favourite motel on the Pacific Coast

Claes Oldenburg, Bedroom
Ensemble 2/3, 1963–69

Highway where every room was decorated with a different animal pattern: the zebra room, the leopard room, etc. One might say that Oldenburg domesticated this artificial zoo by a process of plastification. The project focuses on what Oldenburg described as the 'softest room in the house'.[7] It is an immediate prelude to the better-known work he called 'softies', a series of partially inflated and thus dysfunctional, plastic domestic consumer objects. Like the softies, this psychologically soft room is entirely covered in and partially made of plastic, with the surfaces treated such that every conceivable natural or at least traditional material is imitated – false fur skins abound, marbleised Formica covers the tables and lampshades, the bed is covered in leatherette and the faux Pollocks are made of vinyl. Also like the softies, *Bedroom* uses plastic both actually and virtually: while in one respect all the surfaces imitate other materials and thus exploit plastic's capacity for masquerade, as the sheen of the toilet mimics ceramic, the imitation in *Bedroom* is always incomplete: the photographic images of fur are left flat and smooth, the marbles are in the wrong colours, etc. Thus, the surfaces refer both to their role in simulation and to the characteristics of colourability and smoothness associated with plastic.

But where the dripping solids of the softies suggest a state somewhere between painting and sculpture, the hardness of *Bedroom Ensemble* was clearly meant to suggest architecture. Oldenburg wrote '*Bedroom* might have been called composition for (rhomboids) columns and disks'.[8] Not only was he particularly interested in geometry, which he associated with architecture, but this was the first of his projects to require the technical style of drawing and model-making that approximates the architectural construction or working document. Every detail was worked out in relation to the existing architectural conditions, and he conceived of the process of construction in architectural, indeed Albertian, terms: an 'object made by conventional industrial procedure according to plans by the artist serving his purposes'.[9] As Oldenburg's work entered the sphere of the domestic, into the 'nature of materials' and industrialised modes of production, it seems to have acquired the need for an architectural armature.

But *Bedroom Ensemble* is not traditionally architectural. First of all, there is no room here for inhabitation. *Bedroom Ensemble* may be located in the softest room in the home, yet it is harshly uninviting. The viewer doesn't want to live here, nor can you live in this space lost between motel and gallery, nor does anyone live in this temporary and virtual space, clearly marked private, with the female subject of the leopard-skin coat somehow long gone. Rather than functionally, *Bedroom Ensemble* is architectural insofar as it occupies a position between the plastic and the liberal arts, between a mode of production and a mode of signification. Moreover, it produces a realm between these two and three dimensions and exhibits what one might call dimensional plasticity. The installation is constructed as though it were a perspective drawing, built in a trapezoidal shape with hard edges used to produce the converging lines of a vanishing point. Oldenburg described his work on the *Bedroom Ensemble* as 'upholstering perspective', transforming 'the rationalisation of sight' into a physical fact.[10] In other words, the project is plastic not simply because of the materials used in its construction. More significant is its treatment of the visual field as a moulded and constructed form of material, not as pure projection. *Bedroom* becomes architecture exactly at the moment that it defines itself in relation to both sets of Vitruvian terms: it moulds the image and is thus a plastic art but represents an image and is thus a liberal art.

If *Bedroom* manipulates weaknesses in representational stability to shape for architecture a form of disciplinary plasticity, Archigram performed similar mutations through

35

a kind of technological dissociation. Invoking the operations of disposability, designed obsolescence and nomadic impermanence, the Cushicle produces the plasticity of indeterminacy. The Cushicle is a media-saturated mobile home, a plastic inflatable suit attached to an automotive chassis that permits one to be plugged in and on the move at all times. Designed to be carried by a man on his back, the plastic skins unfold in various configurations, creating at once enclosure, media screens and appliance armatures. A complex prosthetic device, the Cushicle is simultaneously subject and object: when closed it seems, with its spine, head and skin, to be the robotic subject of this itinerant domestic device, but when fully opened the robot who seemed to live in the house becomes the house itself. No other subject seems to be required to watch what is on television in this media architecture: the house watches the screens and goes for a ride in the Cushicle.[11]

Cushicle engages few of the representational issues raised by Oldenburg's *Bedroom*. Instead, it is better understood in relation to the failed attempts to ennoble plastic and to embrace it within a properly defined material peerage. This effort to stabilise the ethical and class structure of materials required arguing that plastic was like other materials, only better.[12] This of course backfired and plastic became characterised not in terms of Wright's notion of aesthetic and structural continuity or of Le Corbusier's ideas about plastic emotions, but in terms of representational imposture. Formica in particular would come to threaten the logical difference between surface and depth, structure and artifice, emerging as a Faustian material that could look like anything and could thus transform all materials into so many arbitrary links in the chain of cultural signification.[13]

This need to find for plastic what Eero Saarinen called 'a proper place in architecture' raised tremendous anxiety – even for Charles Eames, with whom one associates significant plastic production.[14] Saarinen embraced the fully plastic chair, for example in his pedestal chair, but Eames considered plastic a spineless material that offered no resistance. He claimed that you could make terrible mistakes in plastic and felt that its use should be reserved for artists over 50.[15] He was right to try to use plastic as a repository for anxiety about impending old age and developing youth culture, because plastics were in fact becoming the home of the future. In the Monsanto House by Hamilton and Goody and the Smithsons' House of the Future, both of 1957, the continuity of material surfaces, moving from structure to furniture to appliances, enmeshed the architecture with its various prosthetics. Unlike Le Corbusier's notion of equipment, which the Smithsons believed kept equipment hierarchically subservient to the architectural envelope, the moulded plastic shells of these houses of the future appear as residual by-products of the organisation of appliances. Here the plastic arts generate the architecture rather than lie subservient to it, in direct contradiction of the Vitruvian hierarchy. The Cushicle thus relates more to this operational aspect of the Smithsons' Appliance House, which was completely covered in white Formica, than to Oldenburg's insistently exhibitionist focus on the representational falsity of the plastic surface in *Bedroom*. In the hands of Archigram, plastic suggests an architectural epidermis pushed and pulled by the organs of domestic technology.

The softness of these inflatable membranes likened by Banham to human skin relies on the way plastic was becoming a new form of natural tissue. But the soft plasticity of Archigram's bubbles also plays much more specific and strategic architectural roles. The use of foldable, pliable manoeuvrable plastic surfaces permitted the betrayal of architectural categories. In the 'Living 1990' exhibition done by the whole Archigram group in 1967, for example, floors become furniture, furniture turns into walls, walls disgorge robots, all depending on the variable softness permitted by plastic materials. This architectural defiance contrasts sharply with other equally skin-like plastic projects of the era. For example, at the New York 1964 World's Fair many of the corporate pavilions were built of plastic skins. Perhaps most notable among them was Saarinen's IBM pavilion, which had one of the Eameses' multi-screen projects inside. The pavilion was criticised for not being architectural. Instead, it was called environmental, because it allowed for an unregulated flow of visitors and events. Saarinen's use of plastic was essential to this perception, since it was plastic that suggested the mutation of architecture into a new nature developing the organic vocabulary of skins and environments that so captivated Banham.[16]

The Cushicle explored this equivocally architectural status even further. The device was one of a series of Archigram projects conceived as gizmos and gadgets rather than as buildings, such as David Greene's Living Pod or Webb's Suitaloon, a totally personalised environment that could plug into either a Cushicle for mobility or another Suit. The Cushicle is not a building but is simultaneously screen and projection device, immersive image and theatre space, spectator and spectacle. As the skin is broken into disjunctive pieces the observer has no unified image to see, and is not only immersed in the image but is simultaneously caught in the apparatus and technologies of visuality. As the group said about the Living City project, it 'takes the form of a complete structure [and] an organism designed to condition the spectator by cutting him off from the everyday situation, where things are seen in predictable and accepted relationships'.[17] In this sense, the Cushicle plastically defies both technical and disciplinary distinctions between modes of production and modes of representation.

The programmatic and geographical fluidity of these projects, the elastic and cartoon-like quality of the drawings and the treatment of these units as so many disposable consumer commodities lent to the parameters of architecture considerable instability. In fact, when Cushicle was published in *Archigram* 8, the editorial text clearly stated 'we have no buildings here'.[18] What they had instead was plastic shifting between being a kind of material and a form of behaviour. Plastic is thus not hardware or software – terms Archigram introduced in the same issue of their publication that included the Cushicle

– but the indeterminate third term between what they described as tangible, touchable objects and programmatic systems that can be transmitted but not touched. The combination of plastic and plasticity, for Archigram, produced a form of indeterminacy that the group asserted 'threatened the propriety of architectural values', not because it was immoral but because it was amoral.[19]

If *Bedroom Ensemble* and Cushicle acted to plasticise architecture through representational and technical means, Joe Colombo's Total Furnishing Unit, designed for the exhibition at MoMA titled 'Italy: The New Domestic Landscape', used formal and programmatic conditions of homogeneity to similar ends.[20] During the early 1960s, Colombo worked systematically on stand-alone pieces of furniture and domestic appurtenances, including the Universale chair of 1965 and the Boby of 1970. Gradually, however, this emphasis on the design of individual objects gave way to increasingly complex and ultimately self-contained environments. Thus Colombo began with furniture, which became equipment, which became multifunctional appliances that dealt with environments, especially domestic modular units, and which finally became the Total Furnishing Unit, one of the last projects he did before he died.[21]

Although this increased emphasis on environments and programmes would seem to suggest an increased alignment with architecture, the reverse is true. Colombo published an outright assault on architecture titled 'Antidesign'.[22] For Colombo, the hierarchical subordination of furniture to architecture reinforced the separation of modes of production from design and produced a 'confused and disordered habitat filled with a bazaar of disparate objects'. In other words, the cult of the object was the result of architecture's claim to be a spatial art that relegated all else to some lower and uncoordinated status – in other words, that tried to position architecture as a liberal art by distancing itself from the plastic arts. Colombo suggested instead that one begin with the design of the plastic object that produces the space immediately containing the space of living. The result was a kind of ergonomic design that strove to eliminate conventional architecture altogether. The Total Furnishing Unit contains all the necessary requirements, spatial, programmatic and technical, of the modern house, but it lacks the house itself.

Plastic was, for Colombo, the key to this dispossession of architecture, for it alone provided the means needed to eliminate the disciplinary hierarchies on which architecture had thrived. Colombo defined homogeneity as the basic premise underlying his designs, and indeed the individual components of the Total Furnishing Unit are deployed with such density that they suggest almost a homogeneous mass squeezing out any functional space except the basic ergonomic envelope of the body. But more than just their density produces this effect: the almost seamless surfaces of their thermoset plastic repress any indication of joinery and disconnection. Furthermore, while Oldenburg and Webb relied on distinctions between surface and depth, between skin and structure, Colombo's house is almost an uninterrupted piece of plastic, a smooth and semi-solid zone perforated only by the movements of domestic activity.

Modern architects of the 1920s and 1930s eliminated things like mouldings and sculptural treatment from the surfaces of their walls in order to keep dust and other detritus from sticking. In other words, they mobilised a certain notion of hygiene in order to cleanse architecture from its contact with the plastic arts. Colombo, in contrast, totally smothered architecture in plastic, seemingly absorbing the discipline itself into this macromolecular structure. In describing a similar project for the same exhibition, Ettore Sottsass said 'it is a kind of orgy of the use of plastic, regarded as a material that allows an almost complete process of deconditioning from the interminable chain of psycho-erotic self indulgences about "possession"... Ultimately, we feel so detached, so disinterested, and so uninvolved that . . . after a time it fades away and disappears.'[23] The smooth, jointless, textureless surfaces of Colombo's plastic resist all attachment whether in the form of dirt or psychological projection and especially resist the stabilities of architecture.

When a few years after the New Domestic Landscape exhibition Colin Rowe, writing about the New York 5, used the term plastic to describe the physique side of the physique–flesh antithesis, he was restoring exactly the kind of opposition that plasticity was working to undermine.[24] Moreover, Rowe's consistent emphasis on the narrowly architectural belies a different aspect of the work of the 1960s that is important again today, namely the relation of architecture to the plastic and traditionally lesser arts. Just as many of the great designers of plastics began as architects, among them Colombo, Sottsass and Anna Castelli Ferrieri, architecture today is fundamentally unthinkable without its relation to decorative arts, industrial design and fashion. Plastic, moreover, is where all of these cultural practices collide. Rem Koolhaas's work for Prada, for example, relies on plastic as the material and conceptual matrix for cultural and psychological plasticity. When $500 shoes are more noteworthy for their plastic soles than for their leather uppers, one can feel the release from the opposition of real and fake and from what Anna Castelli Fierrieri described as its 'ambiguous association with political protest'.[25] Plastic clothes, plastic displays, programmatic plasticity, plastic money and social plasticity encourage a new kind of disequilibrium: as you shop yourself into an orgy of Prada plastic, even you can mutate into a new form.

If plasticity is now permitting architecture to be reinvigorated rather than tainted by contact with the decorative arts, it is also permitting a new interest in decoration itself to emerge. While buildings like Herzog & de Meuron's Ricola Headquarters are materially plastic, for example, they demonstrate the agility of a plastic decoration that can work through form as well as surface and texture: their box is not only decorated with plastic but in fact uses plasticity to stretch and enfold the moral certainties of such terms. The project, moreover, demonstrates the fluid intermingling of architecture

with graphic design on the one hand and landscape design
at the other extreme, where a photographic impression,
in the case of Herzog & de Meuron, moulds a new
sensibility. Most importantly, if one of the primary
definitions of decoration is that which exceeds, that which
constitutes surplus beyond necessary structure, such
projects are fully excessive. But paradoxically the excess
cannot be excised, for without the superfluity of plastic
there are no projects here.

   With these descriptions we are back to how plastic
operates to dislodge the very disciplinary structure
of architecture. In addition to questions of programme,
decoration and the relation between media, perhaps one
of the most important issues raised by the plasticity of
the contemporary moment involves a radical reorientation
in the notion of architectural space. Rather than an empty
abstraction, the plastic diagram of space describes a
gradual differentiation of material densities ranging
from the invisibility of a gas, to a translucent liquid, to a
solid form. Diller + Scofidio's Blur Building, for example,
transforms glass into a kind of opacity where sight and
space are overcome by the liquid plasticity of the solidify-
ing atmosphere. This capacity to produce these spatial
and optical effects of plastic without any reliance on
the material itself is one of contemporary architecture's
most interesting developments. Indeed, the ultimate
promise of plasticity for architecture lies precisely in its
ability to separate effects from the tyranny of authenticity
arguments, whether related to materials, structure or any
of the panoply of phenomena architecture has misused in
its effort to give the discipline a falsely scientific foundation.
This capacity is not only detachable from materials, it is
also historically portable. Saarinen's TWA terminal, to
use just one example, perfectly instantiates contemporary
effects by its mutation of concrete into a more general form
of plasticity. In fact, while plastic operates to dislodge what
have been accepted as architectural givens, such as the
idea that material specificity, medium specificity and even
semantic specificity are not only linked but all equally

'true' in their own way, the field is also discovering
a disciplinary plasticity that has been latent and that is
being given new urgency.

As demonstrated by this array of diverse projects,
plasticity today obeys no conventional formal or
semiological logic and instead exploits gaps in the
discipline's stabilities to produce experimental sensibilities.
Indeed, for Roberto Unger, plasticity is that which works
against those structures that 'imprison experiments ...
within ... authoritative ideals', of which the discipline of
architecture is a prime example.[26] Instead, plasticity
suggests an architectural behaviour that works towards an
ecology of recombinant productivity. Its efficacy derives,
first, from the fact that not only does plastic lack traditional
material ethics but also from the fact that plasticity is an
unsettling diagram of the negotiation between concept
and materiality. Second, plasticity both constitutes and
exceeds the modern, its fluid agility embodying an aim
that modernity's obsession with structural and formal
regulation repressed. Today, most significantly, plastic's
double status – as a desire to be made and moulded,
as well as a desire to signify – is producing a multivalent
sensibility in which the clarity of view at the core of
the Enlightenment project gives way to the density of
experience. Meaningful without signification, progressive
but not avant-garde, formed but without abjection,
architectural but without hierarchy, plasticity is at the
core of the contemporary architectural project.

First published in Jeffrey Kipnis, Annetta Massie
(eds), *Mood River* (Columbus, OH: Wexner Center
for the Arts, 2002).

FLASH IN THE PAN

NOTES

1. Jean Baudrillard, 'Natural Wood, Cultural Wood', reprinted in Penny Sparke (ed), *The Plastics Age: From Bakelite to Beanbags and Beyond* (Woodstock, NY: Overlook Press, 1993).

2. See, for instance, Roland Barthes' well-known essay first published in his *Mythologies* (Paris: Les Lettres nouvelles, 1957) and reprinted as 'Plastic', *Perspecta* 84 (1988), 92–93.

3. Reyner Bahnham, 'Triumph of Software', in Penny Sparke (ed), *Reyner Banham: Design By Choice* (London: Academy Editions, 1981).

4. Le Corbusier, *Vers une Architecture*, new edition (Paris: G Crès et Cie, 1928), xix and xx.

5. Frank Lloyd Wright, 'In the Nature of Materials: A Philosophy', reprinted in Joan Ockman (ed), *Architecture Culture, 1943–1968: A Documentary Anthology* (New York, NY: Columbia GSAPP/Rizzoli, 1993), 35.

6. Oldenburg rebuilt *Bedroom Ensemble* for the Pop Art exhibition at the Hayward Gallery, London, 1969 and again later that year in his retrospective at MoMA.

7. Cited in Barbara Rose, *Claes Oldenburg* (New York, NY: MoMA, 1970) 193. *Bedroom Ensemble* is often used to mark Oldenburg's shift in attention away from the life of the street and into the home.

8. Cited in Rose, *Claes Oldenburg*.

9. Claes Oldenburg, *The Mouse Museum: The Ray Gun Wing* (Cologne: Museum Ludwig, 1979) 55.

10. Cited in Rose, *Claes Oldenburg*.

11. Cushicle was included in Peter Cook (ed), *Archigram* 8 (1968).

12. See the 1947 issue of *House Beautiful* entirely devoted to plastics.

13. See Ezio Manzini, *The Material of Invention* (Milan: Arcadia Edizioni, 1986).

14. Eero Saarinen, 'On Architecture', in *Saarinen on His Work* (New Haven, CT: Yale University Press, 1962).

15. Cited in Stephen Fenichell, *Plastic: The Making of a Synthetic Century* (New York, NY: Harper Business, 1996).

16. On the 1964 World's Fair, see *Remembering the Future: The New York World's Fair from 1939 to 1964* (New York, NY: Rizzoli, 1989).

17. See 'Living City', in Peter Cook (ed), *Archigram* (New York, NY: Princeton Architectural Press, 1999), 20.

18. See *Archigram* 8, unpaginated.

19. Ibid.

20. Emilio Ambasz (ed), *Italy: The New Domestic Landscape* (New York, NY: MoMA, 1972).

21. For a general overview of Colombo's work, see V Fagone (ed), *I Colombo* (Milan: Mazzotta, 1995).

22. First published in *Casabella* in 1969, the essay is reprinted in *I Colombo*, 219. The essay is often misunderstood as a guilt-ridden attack on the fetishistic attachment to consumer objects created in large measure due to the seductive allure of Colombo's own products.

23. Ambasz, *Italy: The New Domestic Landscape*, 162.

24. Colin Rowe, 'Introduction', to *Five Architects* (New York, NY: Oxford University Press, 1975).

25. See Anna Castelli Ferrieri in Renate Ulmer et al (eds), *Plastics + Design* (Stuttgart: Arnoldsche, 1997) unpaginated insert.

26. See Roberto Unger, *Plasticity into Power* (Cambridge: Cambridge University Press, 1987), 12 and 206–08.

WHAT GOOD IS A BAD OBJECT? (2007)

It has become something of a sport in certain art circles
to go after architecture, to mutilate its body (Monica
Bonvicini likes to go at walls with hammer and axe), abuse
its pantheon (the only way to understand how art criticism
could mistake 'wacky' for a proper critical category is to
acknowledge its scornful hatred of the popular affection for
Frank Gehry), and to literally take up its very space of
existence (everyone loves to love Rachel Whiteread but no
one likes to be the victim of identity theft).[1] So total is this
negative identification with architecture that Benjamin
Buchloh has argued that any radical aesthetic practice
can be such only if it defines itself in a contestatory relation
to architecture.[2] This kind of categorical claim, absolute and
untroubled in its proposition, arouses suspicion. The very
fact that, according to this view, architecture is the source
of radicality in the practices of other mediums – that they
depend on architecture in this important regard – should
be enough to expose that contestation and opposition
are inadequate to define the nature of this relation. The
in extremis of the assertion and the lack of discrimination it
leads to suggest that 'radical' aesthetic practices and their
critics doth protest too much. Indeed, it becomes necessary
not merely to be suspicious of such claims but to understand
them as symptoms – conversion reactions against some
form of intolerable desire.

Incest is, according to Lévi-Strauss, the only universal
taboo. The history of art is riddled with metaphors of
family in the way it describes the relation between the arts:
the arts are sisters, architecture is the mother of all the
arts, and so on. Whatever the particulars of the family unit,
it is a family, even a nuclear family, and too much desire
between its members is unacceptable. Art's attack against

architecture can be read as a defence against too much love, too familiar forms of identification and identity, too much closeness and not enough difference. The violence of the attack, moreover, appears not merely as proper resistance to incest but active fratricide against a rival sibling who has something the other lacks. Envy, worse than jealousy, wracks this sibling who not merely covets, but seeks to destroy, what the other possesses.

The art world has become increasingly predatory in the way it acts out these desires. It has become quite common for art critics to turn their attention to architecture, not so much to convince their readers that there is something to learn from it, but to insist that architecture has managed to usurp public interest that properly belongs only to art and must be reclaimed. The question of art's special interest in architec-ture must be reformulated in light of this kind of rapacious rivalry. What, it has become necessary to ask, does the art world think architecture has that it wants, and wants enough to commit acts of violence? What purpose does such an assault serve? Or even more specifically, how exactly is architecture construed so as to render it deserving of this beating and whose, precisely, are the hands that flagellate? As in any master/slave relation, the dynamic requires that both players are pleasured. And in this particular context, contestatory aesthetic practices appear to be gratified by the pleasure of knowing that architecture deserves what it gets just as architecture has come to enjoy the subservient role. For those forms of art-making defined in opposition to architecture, architecture is an innocent, unselfconscious and sometimes too voluptuous (I think this is what is meant by 'wacky') body that self-evidently requires discipline and to be taught some self-control. For others, architecture is an impersonator that masks its synonymy with corporate enterprise by mimicking the hard-fought innovations of radical sculptural and pictorial practice. Only the lack of intelligence in its apery gives architecture's dissembling away. Architecture requires punishment for its dissimulation and thievery, for not knowing better.

What Buchloh classifies as 'radical aesthetic practices' appear as such because they represent architecture as an idiot savant. Architecture's failure to know, either naive or wilful, makes it possible for other art forms to be 'knowing' in contrast. Indeed, their very radicality relies on producing and then contesting this image of architecture as the overly sexy handmaiden of, and colluding cover for, capital. Criticality, or rather criticality effects and the spectacle of radical resistance, is increasingly produced by staging a combat between art as cunning and architecture as dupe. A complex of phenomena that first began to form during the 1970s, chief among them the emergence of a strong opposition between object and text and hence the conflation of art practice with art criticism, made this criticality effect possible. And already then it significantly relied on construing architecture as the most object-like of objects. In fact, current debates are not only rooted in but are often still raised by practitioners of the 1970s, whose entrenchment in the anti-architecture logic of that period has itself not yet been subject to critique. Even when architecture is chastised for crimes more serious than having indecently expanded beyond what we might call its medium-specific market shares – for example, too happily serving the needs of power – the flagellation fails to account for the guilty pleasure that comes with meting out punishment particularly on the prejudicial basis of class (of objects) rather than specific infractions. At this point it becomes clear that criticality is no longer the result of a specific mode of theoretical analysis and understanding but rather a matter of representation. The techniques of semiotic analysis, once understood as uniquely able to deconstruct the spectacle of representation, are now pressed into the service of a new masquerade. The issue of how and why myriad art forms use architecture as a semiotic stand-in for late capitalism turns out not to be a question of the relation between mediums or of the disciplinary and institutional limits and possibilities they engender. In fact, visual art's love of architecture is not architectural at all but rather turns on the historical status of criticality in the era of spectacle.

This was not always the case. During the late 1960s, advanced cultural forms of all kinds were working through the full impact of the semiotic turn and the regime of the hyper-real, aesthetic practices took pleasure in obfuscating the differences between traditional mediums and disciplines. Rosalind Krauss famously argued that the radicalisation of such practices relied on collusion rather than only on combat.[3] Her schema, however, strictly structuralist at bottom, relied more on difference at its core, making it possible from today's perspective to recognise that the convergence diagrammed by Krauss's expanded field used the fiction of opposition to architecture – what would become today's critical effects – to negotiate transformations that in fact had little to do with architecture at all. If many of the ontologically confusing phenomena of that period – confusing in scale, in function and in duration – were the tools used to think how building and other cultural forms would have to change in the face of the problem of language and the epistemological uncertainties thereby produced, the greatest ontological confusion of this era was not between architecture and other forms of cultural production but between art practice and the practice of criticism itself. Edward Kienholz's *Cement Store* concept tableau and Robert Smithson's *Dearchitecture* projects for LACMA's A&T programme, for example, both worked via the dematerialisation of the architectural object to generate a text-as-work. In both cases, the detour through architecture entailed many steps – from the procurement of materials as resources, their transformation into commodities, their implantation on a site, their ultimate entropy – many more steps than would generally be entailed by other art forms enabling the ensuing text to have much grist for its mill. In other works, architecture functioned as an enormously useful but primarily rhetorical device in the dramatisation of the subsumation of object into discourse. An important result of this process was to make it all too easy for art (both practice and criticism) to present a unified front against architecture.

The shifting relationship between structure and language resonated far beyond discourses of art criticism. Indeed, one of the advances made possible by the ever-widening gap between signifier and signified was the understanding that architecture and the medium of building could be separated. But, as Mark Wigley argued, this realisation seems to have been lost on non-architects, as even Jacques Derrida used architecture as an unexamined and unified sign, and used it naively, no less, as he organised his deconstructing analytic stratagems around classical architecture figures.[4] For architecture, there was and is a great deal at stake in understanding just how the structure part of Derrida's 'Structure, Sign, and Play in the Discourse of the Human Sciences' was understood. Not well, or at least quite literally, seems to be the case, especially in light of the shutdown of productive play between mediums that started to occur between the time the essay was written and finally published in 1970. During these years, Derrida's reading of structuralism expanded into a critique of structurality itself and of the understanding of the centre as not only a repressive concept but an impossible one at that – both bad and false at the same time. As this expansion of the philosophical understanding of structure conflated with post-68 student protests against almost any form of institutional structure as such – as Michel Foucault's virtual diagram of centralising power structures was concretised into physical structures – buildings, which usually contain both structure and centres, began to be identified as the most formidable and obdurate instantiation of economic and political authority. Architecture's objecthood, its physical matter and body, geometry and structure, made it an ideal target. But not because architecture is in fact more complicit or exploitive than other institutions or disciplines, although such claims are easy to make and were all given as reasons. It was an ideal target because it provided highly iconic objects to aim at that consistently resulted in a big show upon impact. Architecture's buildings sat still and were easy to hit, and hitting something – especially if the collision produced a lot of noise – made escaping complicity seem possible. Architecture had become the problem, not a solution, and a straw figure used as a sitting duck in the war against 'the man'.

Another name for a sitting duck is a bad object, which is something that isn't really bad and isn't really an object. Instead, a bad object is a representation, a psychic image that is used to hold and contain all bad things, bad feelings – indeed badness itself. A less technical term is scapegoat. The benefit of producing this bad object is that it makes good objects possible. Good objects and bad objects are equally fictitious: one totally idealised, the other absolutely demonised. Prewar modernists operated in an era of 'truth' and in a culture that perceived architecture as a good object. As such, architecture was idealised and therefore overpromised and underdelivered. In contrast, by the late 1960s, belief in 'the facts' had become the anxious suspicion that necessarily accompanies the regime of representation where nothing can be as it seems. In order to find a significant role in this era, architecture voluntarily committed ritual suicide and provided the social and cultural landscape with a collective bad object.

A good demonstration of how this worked are statements by Julian Beck, the founder of the Living Theatre, a classically avant-garde group that ultimately exiled itself to Europe because its original venues in New York were closed again and again by various government agencies, including the fire department and the IRS. When the NYC building department stepped in, however, Beck's justifiable rage against yet another bureaucracy turned into a rage against architecture itself. The statement was made in the context of a discussion of the 1970 trial of the Chicago Seven, which had become a spectacular event that staged the splitting of the good counter-culture against the bad 'man'. For Beck, architecture organised this split, and what might have been an indictment of the legal system used Mies and his architecture as a theatre on which to stage an attack on repression itself. Beck writes:

During the trial, the judge is annoyed with the defence attorney's unwillingness to sit still. And the judge says, there is a great architect, Mies van der Rohe, who designed that lectern as well as the building, and it was a lectern and not a leaning post. I have asked you to stand behind it when you question the witness.

Pomposity, inflexible, rampant, the tall straight rigid buildings, with the straight proud men, the ramrod spines, not bent by labour ... repressive architecture is rampant... The Parthenon? Its geometry? Beauty and Philosophy are not enough. Who lugged the stones? Who smelted the bronze for van der Rohe's whiskey building? [5]

Over the course of these few sentences, a lectern is transposed into architecture and then into geometry itself, which in turn becomes a system for maintaining not only a repressive legal structure but for social inequity as far back as ancient slavery. In this hysteria, any thought of Mies as a force for good is erased. Such a ramrod slave master could not have been a director of the Bauhaus, a champion of collective housing, a Jew in 1930s Germany who escaped and brought gifts like the Resor House to the US. The use of rigid geometry, for example at the National Gallery in Berlin, to both create impossible new freedoms and to upend the doxa of cultural institutions is beyond consideration. There is no nuance in Beck's diatribe, no sense of the complexities that make up either a person or a building. Mies and his building do not in fact exist for Beck but rather are psychological projections and representations pressed into service as bad objects.

1970 was a good year for being a bad object. Architecture attracted widespread attention for its badness as it became the thing everyone loved to hate. During the Osaka World's Fair, the members of the group EAT convinced themselves that hiding their geodesic dome (military in origin, no less) in a misty fog sculpture would be enough to camouflage the fact that their work was made in and for PepsiCo, as though if you could not see the physical structure (and EAT's dependence on it) the corporation might also disappear. Superstudio thought you could only save architecture by killing it, and in a gesture of utopian mercy they drowned the monuments of Italy. The Austrians and the French preferred to blow things up. Architects willingly served up architecture as a noble sacrifice to the cause. Cutting was a favourite way to demonstrate the badness of the architectural object. Architects transformed the traditional understanding of buildings as bodies into bodies as sites of ritualistic self-mutilation. Peter Eisenman not only sheared the building from architecture and the profession from the discipline but literally cut the Frank House to shreds. The best cutter of them all was Gordon Matta-Clark, who in this same pivotal year of 1970 sliced up a suburban house.

Splitting, the title of Matta-Clark's most influential work, is also the psychoanalytic term for dividing things into good and bad objects. Splitting is a primitive form of defence, useful for infants (and the historical avant-garde), but generally associated with borderline personalities in adults who presumably should be better able to manage a more integrated sense of both good and bad. Splitting is a way of coping with the world that starts off useful and ends up a problem. In 1970, it was good for buildings to get sliced, attacked, blown to bits, hidden and drowned, since the attacks on these bad objects made good political action seem possible. Splitting architecture into a bad object had good purposes, and the structure of representation that made the splitting possible was a needed weapon in a justified war. The refusal to build and the containment of architecture within representation, such as in the work of John Hejduk, was thus not a matter of insufficient opportunity but a matter of principle.

THE FINISHED WORK LASTED THREE MONTHS BEFORE BEING DEMOLISHED FOR URBAN 'RENEWAL'

Gordon Matta-Clark, *Splitting*, 1974

But as is always and inevitably the case, exaggerated moral principles turn into dogma just as in warfare.

Confusion reigns on the battlefield, friendly fire goes off, and the difference between friend and foe gets slippery. Splitting moved from a necessary psychological stage into a pathological condition. Instead of engaging representation as a philosophical question it became an architectural strategy, a space into which architecture moved. By the 1980s, when it became conceivable to some that, for example, Hejduk's Bye House should actually get built, architecture had left the era of representation in and through which Hejduk had conceived the house, to enter a commodified and fetishised space of representation. At this point, representation became a hideout instead of a means of attack.

Today, we can perversely say that we are lucky enough to once again have enemies. The psychological terrain of contemporary culture has shifted: bad objects are everywhere and we don't need to make them up. In fact, we need some, any, good objects. Popular culture is way ahead of architects in recognising and acting on this need. It is eager to love architecture, desperate to perceive it as a good object that always delivers (every celebrity worth their ink in *People Magazine*, from Brad Pitt to Kanye West, seems to want to be an architect). But architects themselves still tend to be self-loathing, ready to reject every accomplishment, embarrassed and perplexed that anyone would think building useful, humiliated and condescending to its own success. That everyone, except architects and art critics, wants to attribute the Bilbao effect to the architect is a good case in point (whatever the facts may be).

These various developments collectively attest to the fact that the contemporary landscape of object relations is shifting. Ironically, if one of the most influential lessons of the 1970s art-as-criticism-of-architecture complex was 'don't judge an object by its form but rather focus on its premises', this also seems to be the lesson that many contemporary art practices are most actively forgetting to learn. From Olafur Eliasson to Anish Kapoor, to name just the two best known examples, artists are certainly not attacking the underbelly of architecture but rather are precisely sampling building's formal qualities with abandon, from its scale and materials to its effects and typologies. On the one hand, the affect of this borrowing is radically different today than it was in the 1970s: the toxic yellow glow of a Bruce Nauman room contrasts sharply with the blushing hues of a Pipilotti Rist interior. On the other hand, artists still presume themselves to have the cultural upper hand, a form of entitlement that enables them to take from architecture without feeling the obligation to say thank you. Kapoor's 2002 *Marsyas* at the Tate, for example, is inconceivable without the research architects have done over the past 20 years in complex geometries, single-surface structures and advanced material fabrication systems but this reliance if not actively repressed is nevertheless certainly unacknowledged.

Such persistent misadventures notwithstanding, architecture is ready to emerge from its hideout in the space of representation: not to return to the impossible ideals of the good object, but to forgo the by-now masochistic pleasure of being a bad object. The question is whether other aesthetic practices are ready to give up the sadistic pleasure that comes from making architecture a bad object. What would 'radical aesthetic practices' look like if they gave up their reliance on beating up buildings in order to produce critical effects or rather to stage and make a spectacle of the effects of criticality? What if the internal landscape of object relations among aesthetic practices was reorganised such that architecture could be what Winnicott called the good-enough object, an object good at some things in some contexts for some period of time for particular purposes.[6] Instead of assuming that architecture knows nothing about itself, either through wilful denial or just plain stupidity, is it now possible to conceive that architecture already knows some things – things that might be of interest to other forms of aesthetic practice?

What's good enough about architecture today is that it is pushing beyond conventional forms of radicality based in the spectacle of opposition and combat to produce new forms of radical engagement. The most interesting of contemporary architecture is the product of contamination: use and exchange value, event and image, resistance and capitulation, control and freedom. And it is ultimately this capacity not only to be but to withstand being just good enough, to tolerate the compromises that accompany real action in the world and to relinquish the confidence that accompanies accepting no less than utopian absolutes that architecture has and that other aesthetic practices envy. This capacity to hold simultaneously and together opposing feeling states rather than merely to split and contest is the basis of this newly embedded radicalism and is what good enough architecture has to offer today.

First published in *Volume* 13 (2007)

NOTES

1. Hal Foster, *Design and Crime and Other Diatribes* (New York, NY: Verso, 2002), 35.

2. Benjamin Buchloh, 'Cargo and Cult: The Displays of Thomas Hirschhorn', *Artforum International*, November 2001, 107–08.

3. Rosalind Krauss, 'Sculpture in the Expanded Field', in Hal Foster (ed), *The Anti-Aesthetic* (Port Townsend, WA: Bay Press, 1983), 31–42.

4. Mark Wigley, *The Architecture of Deconstruction: Derrida's Haunt* (Cambridge, MA: MIT Press, 1993).

5. Julian Beck, *The Life of the Theater; The Relation of the Artist to the Struggle of the People* (San Francisco, CA: Limelight Editions, 1972), unpaginated.

6. DW Winnicott, 'Transitional Objects and Transitional Phenomena', *International Journal of Psychoanalysis*, 1953, 89–97.

WHAT COLOUR IS IT NOW? (2004)

'The twentieth century' is full of blueness: from the primary blue of De Stijl, to International Klein Blue, to the famous Blue Meanies populating the world of the Beatles' Yellow Submarine. But it is one particular hue that underlies modernity itself: cathode ray blue. More than just a colour, cathode ray blue is a machine-made effect, not only itself denaturalised but a force that denaturalises the atmosphere as it moves from machine by-product to the plane of perception. Cathode ray blue negotiates between technology and effect in such a way as to render it an especially useful cipher for the discipline of architecture, where colour has historically been treated either as pure signifier or repressed altogether. Cathode ray blue works more as an impression than a pigment, more to produce mood than meaning. None of the many available analytiques of colour, which range from the psycho-physiological to the phenomenological, from the semiological to classifying colour as a social practice, are adequate to understanding these effects: the impulse to codification fails to suggest how and why cathode ray bluism is not a colour but diagrams the very affect of contemporary architecture.[1] Cathode ray blue is thus the ideal starting point for a new theorisation of colour in architecture, one that leaves the limitations and imperatives of signification behind.

To pivot from the meaning of colour to its effects, we recognised that the main effect produced by colour is the effect of today. Today, in this sense, is not just a moment in time but a feeling state produced by the passage of things in the world through the sensory apparatus until they form apperceptions. Colour is important now because it provides a means for considering how phenomena produce effects beyond themselves (in the case of colour beyond its physical confines in space, beyond the science of its pigmentation and beyond the meanings it has been assigned by culture) and for understanding the role of these effects in establishing the affective environment of the contemporary. Colour effects contemporary affect or what Charles Baudelaire described as presentness.[2] For Baudelaire, the key indicators of presentness were the mannerisms of everyday life and fashion in particular. The more extreme the expression of these qualities the more presentness was invoked. Thus, for Baudelaire, the prostitute was an exceptionally contemporary figure because she was exaggeratedly mannered and overdressed. 'The black with which the eye is outlined, and the rouge with which the upper part of the cheek is painted', he wrote, conjured what he called a 'supernatural and excessive life' and it is this combination of colour, artifice and exaggerated-ness that enable time to imprint on the senses. In other words, colour is the valence of the present and cathode ray blue was, at the turn of the twenty-first century, what red and black was to the nineteenth-century prostitute.[3]

Insofar as it marks the point where colour meets technology and produces of the conjunction the effect of the contemporary, cathode ray blue could actually be said to predate the cathode ray by at least half a century. In fact, the first architectural manifestation of cathode ray blue was actually and ironically made out of glass. Even though most modernist accounts of glass describe an absence of material and colour not meant to produce the prostitute's presentness, when a lot of glass was used, when glass itself was as exaggerated as a prostitute's rouge, her tempting flicker of provisionality appeared nevertheless. Consider this account of the Crystal Palace, perhaps the most historic locus of the architecture of technological effects, colour and blue, 'If we let our gaze travel downward it encounters the blue-painted lattice girders . . . they are interrupted by a dazzling band of light . . . which dissolves into a distant background where all materiality is blended into the atmosphere.'[4] The Crystal Palace, in addition to the many transcendental truths modernism asked it to speak, was enormously 'effective', a tour de force of dazzlement and a special effects machine.[5] Blue, not in its specific guise as symbol of modernity and its technologies but rather as a stand in for colouration that works on the surface of buildings, in this case across the girders, through the glass and into the air itself, constituted the binding medium of this atmospheric perspective. Not true blue but colour as a material instrument of effects generated the ineffable qualities in the Crystal Palace that during the nineteenth century were thought to have been brought into architecture by nothing less than sparkle-producing fairies.[6]

Like all technologies that can go from novel to obsolete in the blink of an eye, cathode ray blue hinges between two views of colour, one increasingly outdated not only by its association with by-gone technologies like fairies and curtain walls but by its entrenchment in the logic of the sign. The other view of colour seeks the effects of presentness and requires – ironically – a deeply historical understanding of past discourses on colour's relationship to architecture and the visual arts. Despite architecture's long and well-known problem with polychromy, the discipline has in fact succeeded in largely ignoring the issue of colour as such.[7] But in art historical and rhetorical discourses, colour has engendered an elaborate theoretical apparatus that revolves precisely around the link between sensibility and intellection, in other words around colour's relationship to affect.[8] By even briefly examining this apparatus, it becomes apparent that the long tradition in architecture of subjugating colour to meaning, need not preclude the possibility of developing for architecture a less 'meaningful' but more effective sense of what it can do in and through colour. It only makes the embrace of the colour more new and more clearly connects colour not to the vagaries of technological currencies but to the contemporary itself.

The primary art historical formulations on the subject took place in the context of the debate between *colore* and disegno, in fact a conflict over whether painting should be *organised* around meaning or affect.[9] By refusing to take part in this debate, architecture by default sided with *disegno*, entirely aligning its discipline with the regulations of design, so that the possibilities of *colore* barely inflect the field, even when its buildings have been significantly coloured. Since the Renaissance, architecture has been constituted in the act of design and through the medium of the drawing and both were established specifically against colour. Even though when Brunelleschi made his gadget depicting the Florence Baptistery it was the thrilling and coloured verisimilitude that made people gasp, architecture as a field has remembered only the orthogonals of his perspective drawing.

The overdetermination of architecture by design is characterised by two trajectories that were coterminous for Brunelleschi but progressively diverged as the uses of drawing proliferated. The world that was captured by Brunelleschi's device was both real and ideal. On the one hand, Brunelleschi's drawing subjected the real world of Florence to the strictures of mathematical regularity, and thereby inaugurated a certain form of the pursuit of realism in architectural drawing. On the other hand, the same mathematical regulation permitted the drawing to be received not as a representation of reality but as the manifestation of an idea conceived, however divinely, by the architect. It was this ideality that was used to authorise architecture's entry into the world of the liberal arts and thus to equate the architect with the visionary artist.

The provocation of this conflict internal to the origins of perspective relatively quickly gave way to isolating the two trajectories. Thus, the intellectual nature of perspective gave architecture the capacity to envision new worlds with the authority of the ideal in the technical sense of the term and this idealism under-girds much visionary drawing, whether rendered in perspective or not. At the same time, perspective forever yoked architectural drawing to the rules of mathematical accountability, and thus the drawing became, as importantly as it became the vehicle of imagining, the legal instrument of the profession. The whole apparatus of working drawings, construction documents and so forth, even though not drawn in perspective (in fact usually perspective is explicitly forbidden), can be traced to the faith in perspective's capacity to constitute the real. Perspective is in that sense a perfect example of an ideological instrument, and not just what Erwin Panofksy called a world view, because it hegemonically offers itself as a means of representation that is so complete that it spans the spectrum from the real to the ideal and can even engulf drawings not explicitly rendered in perspective.

As the development of digital drawing seems to be continuing the will to perspective by dividing itself between the professional labours of CAD drafting on the one hand, and the voluptuous fantasies of rendering and modelling softwares on the other, it might be productive to think that the collapse of *disegno* into perspective was not the only possibility for architecture. And for the sake of my argument, let us equate this opposition with the limitation of architecture not to black and white but to green – the code colour for 'in the nature of materials' and thus for reality – and pink – the proverbial rose-tinted glasses.

In painting, by contrast, the question of drawing was framed quite differently. There, drawing, or rather *disegno*, was not dominated by controversies between the real and the ideal but rather was concerned with drawing as a mode of imitation, of which there were many kinds. *Disegno* was primarily differentiated from *colore*, which was understood as a technique of affect rather than of mimesis. From the sixteenth century on, as the relative merits of Michelangelo and Titian, Poussin and Reubens, Ingres and Delacroix were debated, *disegno* and *colore* were compared as modes of pictorialism. *Disegno* was linked primarily to a representational and narrative-driven paradigm, whether hyperrealistic or super-idealised, while *colore* was associated with the world of affect and sensation. It was thus colour that was said to make 'painting seem alive' and that could 'commonly ravish our sight with the bewitching pleasure of delightsome and stately ornaments'.[10] While it was precisely the intoxicating quality of colour that led theorists to be afraid of its charms, as they feared a seductive temptress, one wonders what might have happened to architecture had it succumbed to the temptation and allowed its 'design' to engage the antithetical pleasures of depiction not authorised by perspective.

For its own purposes – entry into the liberal arts, establishing a base in professionalism, guaranteeing the permanent monumentality of its built output – architecture remained largely contained within what we could call intra-drawing issues, leaving matters of colour to the side. The theoretical underpinnings of the late-eighteenth- and nineteenth-century architectural discussions about polychromy, for example, stem primarily from a concern with the representation of antiquity: for Quatremère de Quincy, colour is a sign of classicism and in that sense Quatremère is concerned with colour as a component of imitation rather than with its affective role.[11] And while arguments about the polychrome condition of ancient statues of Athena would seem quite distinct from the use of colour by Le Corbusier, for example, the theoretical underpinnings are related. For Le Corbusier, colour is used as a notational system and as a means of formal codification. Modernism in general used colour to clarify and elucidate both the formal and technical aspects of its kit of parts. It can therefore be argued that both Quatremère and Le Corbusier used colour for representational rather than affective purposes and thus produced coloured 'designs' rather than designs in colour. Only when factors outside the confines of the discipline came to the fore – as was the case with the Crystal Palace, which was not designed by an architect strictly defined, was conceived outside the conventional strictures of both the profession and its typical programmes, and was made within a milieu of licentiousness created most obviously by its excessive use of a single material – could modern architecture tolerate a swerve towards *colore*.

Because architecture pressed even colour into the service of *disegno*, imagining architectural design in colour is, by disciplinary definition, a transformational proposition. *Colore* can as a result be used to reconfigure the origins of architectural 'design' in perspective and to loosen the grip of *disegno* on the discipline. More specifically, colour can be made to emerge as having increasingly become a tool in the production of architectural presentness. Temporality, and thus the form of presentness that generally goes by the name 'modernity', first became of concern in relation to colour when artists sought to distinguish historical or visionary events from current events. *Grisaille*, a monochrome palette of greys, was used during the Renaissance to signify the pastness of antiquity while polychromy was reserved specifically for the depiction of the present. While a *grisaille* painting could incorporate elements of colour to indicate a form of contemporaneity, it did so by symbolising modernity, not by considering the use of colour in relation to effects, whether of contemporaneity or of other kinds. On the other hand, time and colour, even monochromy in particular, came together in what was perhaps the first attempt to identify architecture as a field of special effects. For Wölfflin, most notably, the chiaroscuro that was generated by the dynamics of light moving across a variegated surface gave Baroque architecture its 'painterly' as opposed to linear quality. Painterliness was thus characterised for Wölfflin by atmospheric effects rather than by modes of imitation and was intensified by animation rather than by chromatic polemics: the dynamics of a small range of tones was more effective in his view than extreme variations in colour, or mere colourfulness. 'Vitality', 'incidental effects', 'broken surfaces' and 'atmospherics' rather than a specific palette were the techniques he identified as being able to engage architecture in the speculative and effective terrain of *colore*.[12]

Wölfflin thus demonstrates that colour is not merely a palette or a pigment; it is a means of engaging the territory of effects. And the more effective the colour, the more able it is to convey presentness. Colour becomes contemporary as it moves away from indexicality, symbolism, codification and ideation, because this move away from signification allows colour to register traces of a much more complex series of historically specific conditions and forces: those of technology, sensibility, capital, taste, materiality, manufacture. In other words, when working through the field of effects, colour can do more to engage contemporaneity than when it works through the structures of meaning.

Two distinct techniques in the use of colour, what I will call Wallpaper Colour and the Hyperpainterly, are proving to be most effective in broadening the range of effects available to architecture, reinventing the field's horizon of possibilities and encouraging architecture to engage the contemporary. Wallpaper Colour works through extreme scale, environmental saturation and the hypergraphical. Sometimes incorporating pattern, Wallpaper Colour is always flat and superficial. It is not in the nature of materials, but rather acts as a varnish suffusing architecture with ambient effects. Wallpaper Colour immerses the viewer in the atmospheres of dimensional chromaticism but does not give up notational clarity altogether. This inherent contradiction can be seen in the mid-century collaborative project by André Bruyère and Fernand Léger, the *Village Polychrome*, which used Wallpaper Colour to elide architecture with painting and landscape even though paint charmingly codified

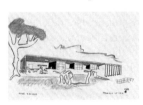

notions of formal propriety. In the supergraphics in postmodern architecture by figures such as Charles Moore and Venturi Scott Brown Wallpaper Colour was employed to deliberately disobey formal codification while retaining an emphasis on legible signage. These examples underscore one

André Bruyère and Fernand Léger, Village Polychrome, 1953

of the most important effects of Wallpaper Colour, which is to move architecture away from the design of space and toward the production of zones or environmental moods.

The Hyperpainterly focuses on the surface effects of animate colour in the production of contemporaneity. Like Wallpaper Colour, the Hyperpainterly works through

extreme scale and environmental saturation. But unlike
Wallpaper Colour, the Hyperpainterly does not rely
on graphic or uniform colour. Instead, the Hyperpainterly
is a flavour and an additive that gives vibe to the surface
through patterned shifts and tonal variations of colour.
If Wallpaper Colour manages notational codification, the
Hyperpainterly manages affective codification, avoiding
a too obvious and limiting reliance on associations
between colour and feelings. Herzog & de Meuron use
the Hyperpainterly to produce what could be called the
atmospherics of Impressionism, for example. But Herzog
& de Meuron eliminate the sentimental and naturalistic
associations of the impressionist colour palette to retain
only its cloudy indeterminate quality. A collaborative
proposal for the Caltrans Headquarters submitted
by Rem Koolhaas and John Baldessari transfigures Los
Angeles into a mechanically mobilised form of pointillism:
individual trucks painted in different colours act like
semi-autonomous pixels, colonising the city each day
in a variegated pattern with their mood-inducing colours.
Herzog & de Meuron also worked with an artist (Michael
Craig-Martin) when developing the colour scheme for the
Laban Dance Centre, suggesting that colour is a means of
expanding not only architecture's range of effects but also
the discipline and its limits through collaboration with
other disciplines. While these projects might also indicate
that architects need to hire a colour 'expert' because such
expertise is still seen as the domain of the artist, some
of Frank Gehry's work indicates that this need not be the
case. The iridescent pink of his Canadian Winery, and the
manipulation of the titanium of Bilbao or Disney Concert
Hall to exaggerate monochromatic chiaroscuro effects,
suggests that hyperpainterliness is an architectural effect
and not a product of architects.

Whether in the form of Wallpaper or the Hyperpainterly, colour puts architecture in the mood of today.
Colore may always have belonged properly to the field
of effects rather than to the field of signification, but it has
not always had the effect of the now. In the modern period,

the period that invented the problem of the now, colour has become increasingly embedded in issues of technology, mass culture and the global market. Many lament the age of authentic colour when architecture was always in some sense green – in the nature of materials (and their various colours). But the redness of brick or the whiteness of whitewash, while perhaps full of eternal values of some kind, have none of the timeliness of avocado Formica or the Pantone chip *du jour*. Precisely because of colour's mediation by colour experts, industrial trends and the mechanisms of designed obsolescence by virtue of the material, technical and cultural emulsion through which it operates, colour is the most implicated phenomenon in both architecture's current affectiveness and its *effectiveness*. Finally, because effects are now important agents in the production of political and cultural change, architecture can choose to use colour to expand its role in shaping the sensibility that is today.

First published in *Perspecta* 35 (2004)

NOTES

1. A vast amount of literature on the history and theory of colour exists beyond the scope of this essay. Nevertheless, it is essential to acknowledge Mark Wigley's *White Walls, Designer Dresses, The Fashioning of Modern Architecture*, (Cambridge, MA: MIT Press, 1995), David Batchelor's *Chromophobia* (London: Reaktion, 2000) and *Colour* (Cambridge, MA: Whitechapel/MIT Press, 2008).

2. Sylvia Lavin, 'The Temporary Contemporary', in *Perspecta* 34 (2003), 128–38.

3. Charles Baudelaire, trans Jonathan Mayne, *The Painter of Modern Life and other Essays*, (London: Phaidon, 1964).

4. Cited in Sigfried Giedion, *Space, Time and Architecture* (Cambridge, MA: Harvard University Press, 1941), 252.

5. This aspect of the Crystal Palace has generally been discussed in the context of the technological sublime.

6. On the particular identification of blue with modernity, see Michel Pastoureau, *Blue: The History of a Colour* (New York, NY: Princeton University Press, 2001).

7. On the history of polychrome in architecture, see David van Zanten, *The Architectural Polychromy of the 1830s* (New York, NY: Garland, 1977). For an analysis of modernity's repression of colour in architecture, see Mark Wigley, *White Walls*.

8. For an extensive bibliography on colour in art, see John Gage, *Color and Culture: Practice and Meaning from Antiquity to Abstraction* (Berkeley, CA: University of California Press, 1993).

9. For an analysis of this debate, see Jacqueline Lichtenstein, *La Couleur éloquente: Rhétorique et peinture à l'age classique* (Paris: Champs/Flammarion, 1989).

10. F Junius, *De pictura veterum* (Amsterdam, 1634); English translation as The Painting of the Ancients (London, 1638).

11. Sylvia Lavin, *Quatremère de Quincy and the Invention of a Modern Language of Architecture* (Cambridge, MA: MIT Press 1992).

12. Heinrich Wölfflin, *Renaissance and Baroque*, trans Kathrin Simon (Ithaca, NY: Cornell University Press, 1964), 34–36.

VANISHING POINT (2012)

The pavilion is everywhere in the contemporary cultural
landscape. Indeed, these structures are one of the few
species on this terrain whose numbers are growing.
While such growth is normally understood to signal the
health of an ecosystem, the abundance of the pavilion
today instead signals the end of an era – and a new kind
of ending, one that challenges our modes of evaluating
cultural production as a whole.

Confronting endings has long been a central
function of criticism: this task has been essential to art
and architectural history since the modern fields began.
From Johann Joachim Winckelmann's notion of decline to
today's understanding of the limit conditions of possibility,
endings have been assumed to result naturally from a
loss of cultural relevance and so have played a more pivotal
role than beginnings in understanding historical change.
Yet theories of endings have also been used to privilege
the new. For example, Heinrich Wölfflin made his classic
distinction between the linear and the painterly in neutral
but comprehensive terms; one was not better than the other,
but each described inescapable historical forces limiting
the options available to artists and architects at a given time.
For him, linear work made in a painterly period constituted
an aberration, a category error. But a corollary to this
historical structure was the high value he placed on objects
that anticipated impending change; the gothic shoe foretold
the naturalism of the Renaissance, in his view, and so was
celebrated for its proleptic function. Decreasing numbers
thus proved the loss of dominance of a set of aesthetic
operations as surely as the *rara avis*, alone but ahead,
foretold a swell in alternate modes of production and so
proved the always self-correcting vigour of the zeitgeist.

But this situation has now changed entirely. In the complex ecology that characterises our contemporary culture of excess, we can no longer assume that a population will die out simply because it has lost its connection to the most pressing issues of the day. Paradoxically, evidence of irrelevance instead lies in overproduction and superexposure: a new typology now waxes when it is on the wane.

Pavilions are being constructed, assembled, installed and jerry-rigged in astonishing and rapidly increasing numbers. Schools have students build them, museums have young architects compete to design them, and pop-up pavilions are rapidly becoming a favoured form of retail space. Individual pavilions become famous, with collectors lining up to buy them and blogs tracking every step of their often brief lives. The sheer quantity of pavilions built the world over is staggering, but perhaps even more impressive is the equally vast assortment of institutions, arts programmes, biennials and expos that commission them. This dazing proliferation of pavilions indicates not only a general cultural change but a significant shift in the architectural discipline. As a building type, the pavilion has never had a prescribed function and is typically a temporary structure. But more important than the actuality of their relatively short life spans is the fact that the absence of the demand to endure made room for pavilions to prioritise visual effects over and against typical architectural stabilities: pavilions, at least in the early era of their proliferation in eighteenth-century gardens, often lacked plumbing, foundations and cultural gravitas such that even when all three ultimately became present, as they often were in the nineteenth century, the pavilion maintained conceptual lightness and flexibility.

This genealogy, which encouraged the pavilion often to assume an intensely aesthetic posture, made the pavilion an ideal site for architectural experimentation, and it has perhaps never served this function quite so well as during the early twentieth century. Arguably, the pavilions of this era shaped future architecture more than permanent buildings, because their very temporariness freed them from prevailing habits, enabling them to materialise concepts not yet readily available. For example, Le Corbusier's 1924 Esprit Nouveau Pavilion made plausible what had hitherto been merely a hypothetical scenario for living. A proposal for a radically new way of life, in which domesticity in every respect was to be restructured, may well have been easy to ignore in a drawing, revealing the proposal as precisely what it was – a projection. Building the proposal, however, though the building was just as projective as a drawing would have been, took advantage of the 'reality effect' that architecture so easily achieves at full scale. Because the structure is real (it stands up, can be entered and keeps the rain out), the suggestion is made that its proposal is real as well. In this way the Esprit Nouveau Pavilion functioned as a built manifesto for the future, as a means of making the present appear to enter the future. Similarly, Ludwig Mies van der Rohe's famous Barcelona Pavilion, whose glass box seemingly hovered in a fairground otherwise covered in weighty monuments at the 1929 International Exposition, presaged the development of a media-driven culture not only insofar as its legacy was propagated more through the weightlessness of photographs than through the material of the building but also because of the way it interpolated this future dematerialisation in its very design. Both these pavilions may have lacked typical architectural programmes, but they both were programmed with and for the future. The pavilion was the Wölfflinian gothic shoe of the early twentieth century.

But at a certain point in the twentieth century, the pavilion's temporary status ceased to be an exceptional position of privilege and began to blend in with the mania for trends, planned obsolescence and obsession with the new that characterised postwar consumer culture. What these developments meant for the pavilion in particular was made clear by John McHale's now famous 1966 essay, 'The Plastic Parthenon', in which he adds to Walter Benjamin's reflection on the impact of mechanical modes of reproduction on works of art the question: what impact will mechanically generated modes of *ephemeral*

reproduction have on works of art. Not only was unique-
ness and authenticity now on the chopping block of mass
culture but so was permanence, whether situated in a
utopian past, the home of the Parthenon, or in a fantastical
future, presumably to be made all in plastic. Indeed, for
McHale the past and the future may have saved a place
for permanence but the present was only a diffuse and
continuous flow of mass quantities of replications operating
through shiftlessness in medium and mustering importance
only through sheer numbers. In this context, once radical
because ephemeral works of the avant-garde were at risk of
being easily consumed in the cultural marketplace and of
being reduced to objects characterised by mere transience.

McHale argued that an excessive quantity of
ephemeral replicas of icons, in other words a massive
stream of images of endurance, actually undid rather
than reinforced permanence. (As much as he understood
obsolescence to be the condition of this present, McHale
understood the work of the avant-garde to be resisting
this condition, ephemerality having gone from critique
of bourgeois culture to instrument of consumer culture.
In other words, however ironically and distinct from the
needs of today, McHale's analysis of ephemera was made in
order to salvage a notion of endurance.) The contemporary
pavilion has reached precisely this moment of reversal
of effect and exhaustion of potential: rather than radicalise
the contemporary, the pavilion as provisional experiment
in the nature of ephemerality has successfully produced
a market for 'the contemporary pavilion'. Today,
contemporaneity is a programme, a market value and
an opportunity for professional advancement, the most
powerful evidence of this commodification of the
contemporary being the fact architectural pavilions now
constitute their own niche within (rather than outside,
posed critically against) professional practice. The result is
that while firms specialising in hospital or stadium design
would once have been understood to be separated from
pavilion architects by a vast ideological divide, today they
increasingly operate in accordance with the same values

of efficiency, service and art as added value. Furthermore, even though the pavilion is still reflexively associated with experimental projects, its camouflaged historicism places it fundamentally at odds with advanced modern ambitions. For example, Jürgen Mayer H's 2011 Metropol Parasol in Seville, one of many recent not-quite-buildings, exploits the historically progressive attributes of the pavilion – artful compositional looseness, the visual openness of garden structures, and even the image of immediacy (the egg-crate structure of the Parasol evokes a common technique used by architects to make models in paper) – to mask a regressive urban intervention with a massive scale and dense programme, permanence and infrastructure reminiscent of a monumental nineteenth-century train station. While the size of their population is indicative – and can in fact teach us much about why they flourish – today's pavilions are no longer proleptic, having lost any connection to an advanced cultural or historical project. Without a teleological motivation rooted in the belief that architecture's role is to realise the zeitgeist, these 'pavilionised' buildings cannot function as an index of disciplinary ambition for the future. The pavilion is thus simultaneously an acutely contemporary symptom of the forces shaping our cultural landscape and, perhaps more provocatively, an anachronism.

The pavilion's fall from project to party décor is making odd bedfellows of once-estranged parts of the architectural world – an interbreeding that results in a weakened version of architecture. Ironically, the ascendancy of the pavilion in the art world may be in part a predatory response to that very weakness, as architecture in this enfeebled state is increasingly susceptible to takeover by a new kind of hybrid art practice. Indeed, the principal source of the pavilion's overproduction is the almost viral fecundity of the complex ecology that has come to characterise current relations between art and architecture. While pavilions were traditionally within the purview of architects, today they are equally likely to be made by artists, architects or both working in collaboration. In part the pavilion's proliferation is simply due to this expanding population of producers, but it is even more fundamentally linked to the changing nature of the relationship between art and architecture. The two fields have always been related (both conceptually and, more literally, through direct collaboration), but sometimes this connection is only casual or coincident to their shared status as liberal arts. At other times, art and architecture intertwine in more profound ways. For example, theories of mimesis linked the arts for centuries, but when the invention of perspective cut a window onto the pictorialisation of nature, it both unified representation and – in the form of this window – created a threshold of difference separating art and architecture from each other and from the world. Recognising the very differences between architectural and other forms of imitation became essential for understanding this development. The window's multiple ontology as architectural element, conceptual scheme, representational frame and philosophical structure served as the means by which multiple systems worked themselves into order. It was, in other words, the vehicle through which perspective became an episteme rather than merely a visual device.

The state of the contemporary pavilion can be traced back to another acute moment of change in the relations between art and architecture, when, in the 1970s, the room rather than the window was the vehicle for ontological recalibration. A notion of the 'real' became the era's perspective: a symbolic form, an epistemological regime, and a diagram of power. At this point, artists and architects made different claims about how to understand the real, which rested on different conceptions of the room. Both rejected the pictorialism of the window, favouring what was then understood as the more phenomenologically and socially robust conditions offered by the space of a room. But artists argued that to act on the room – by sitting directly on its floor, exposing the studs in its walls or peeling off drywall and tar paper and paint – was to leave a trace in the world rather than to construct an image of it.

As a result, they sought rooms that could be presented as coterminous with the real – building in a state of nature, hence their preference for lofts, factories and other raw industrial spaces in a postindustrial world. For this staging to succeed, the room had to be distanced from architecture, then cast as a bad object, the institution to be critiqued and a prison of language – the apex of structure and modernist rationality imposed onto some purer, prelinguistic state of the real.

Meanwhile, architects were doing precisely the reverse, developing architectural theory as opposed to buildings, focusing on semiotics, distancing architecture from the mundane realities of building, and working especially hard to turn architecture into language and thereby earn autonomy, divesting themselves of the inarticulateness of building. Within the architectural discipline, the raw room favoured by art appeared to be an unattainable utopian fantasy of the precultural. Architecture sought instead the reverse utopia, a purely cultural sphere from which all economic and other contaminants of the 'real' were evacuated, and for this they needed a room as close to a virtual envelope as could be constructed: a room for the unreal.

And so a notion of the real – which Rosalind Krauss, writing at the time, called 'sensuous immediacy' and Dan Graham, speaking of his own pavilions, referred to as the 'actual' – became the primary art/architectural separatrix of the era and in fact still haunts the production and reception of pavilions today. Indeed, just as the window in part determined the problem of the room, the room in turn shaped the horizons of the pavilion. In 1967, when Carl Andre was installing his 'Cuts' in the single-room Dwan Gallery in Los Angeles, covering its entire floor with flat concrete bricks, he made a drawing (used for the exhibition poster) that reversed the voids and the bricks. In other words, even when his work was doubly mediated and looking like an architectural artefact – it was technically now a floor plan represented on a printed poster – Andre seemed to conceive of it as a photographic negative, the plane of the world on which the bricks had left a physical imprint. That same year, Peter Eisenman began work on the Barenholtz Pavilion, later known as House 1, which was also in effect a single room, but a room without actuality: here there was no programme to control the use or deployment of space (its original function was to display a small collection of antique toys), no site peculiarities to determine massing, no context requiring response. And the more than 300 drawings Eisenman made for the project reveal an obsession to evacuate any and all traces of the actual world – its toilets, its human subjects, its gravity, its building – to leave only what he called 'a new mental image of an environment different from that which we are actually seeing', or what amounted to his understanding of architecture. While artists were resisting the commodification of art by emphasising the built room as an instantiation of real material conditions, literal experience and direct means of construction, architects rejected the reality of programme and structure that would inevitably lead to commodification, instead simplifying architecture into a virtual pavilion.

This dynamic between artists treating the room as real space and architects striving for the room as an ideated world initiated a period in which the material products of art and architecture began to approximate each other, first in scale and then through other means. What eventually emerged was not only a shared space, but also a connecting zone into which both disciplines could enter, a kind of air lock controlling the passage between two isomorphic but incompatible environments. The result was the transformation of the pavilion into an intellectual project through which were negotiated the relations between materials and forms, the components of modern mediums in which specificity distinguished architecture from other arts, and the relations between procedures and techniques such as drawing, repetition and other features of postmodern disciplinary overlap. A chart tracing the development of this model could follow Andre's 'Cuts' and Eisenman's cubes with the landmark 1976 exhibition

'Rooms' at PS1 Contemporary Art Center (now MoMA PS1) in New York. Here, building as medium was sundered from architecture as discipline in a series of works made principally through the often dramatised removal, displacement and repurposing of building detritus.

A quarter century later, the 1999 'Predator' pavilion by Greg Lynn and Fabian Marcaccio explored the kinds of postmedium collaboration newly engendered by the use of digital tools across mediums.

Greg Lynn and Fabian Marcaccio, *The Predator*, Frankfurt, 1999

Using massive digital printers and computer-guided mills, the plastic panels of the pavilion walls and the images covering them were computer-generated, printed and vacuum-formed as a single entity to produce a material index of the collapse of medium-specific rationales. And yet Marcaccio applied a thick impasto to the shell's surface by hand just as Lynn used a deliberately rough assembly of twist ties to structure the panels – reasserting disciplinary distinction, manual labour and material values at the very moment that digital-fabrication tools seemed to dissolve them. A few years later still, in 2003, François Roche of R&Sie Architects, Philippe Parreno and Rirkrit Tiravanija put together Hybrid Muscle, one of many pavilions that comprise Tiravanija's and Kamin Lertchaiprasert's *Land* project in Thailand. Harnessed to a water buffalo, this diaphanously skinned skeletal frame with movable wings was a biotechnical apparatus designed to generate power for cell phones in the local community. Here the pavilion was reterritorialised as the generator of a diverse art-architecture ecology where 'culture' and the 'actual world' cohabitate.

But these productive, postmedium investigations into pavilion, structure and environment are the exception. While Hybrid Muscle imagines the eventual disappearance of building and architecture into environment, a complex reimagining of culture and ecology, mostly we see one pavilion after another, a never-ending 'pavilionisation' spreading into a homogenised field of cultural production. On the one hand, the pavilion is the apotheosis of installation art, now so conceptually expansive that its ultimate medium is necessarily a small building (that must therefore meet accessibility codes). On the other, architectural design has been largely reduced to pavilion making, as the economic collapse has meant that few can afford anything but a tiny building (and are glad not to have to pay for plumbing). These trajectories explain a number of shifts: take Frank Stella's move from canvas, to canvas in 3D, to 3D container for painting in his unrealised design for the Costantini Museum, or, more broadly, the material and conceptual shrinking of architecture from complex and manifold structure to politically eviscerated shed, as exemplified by Oscar Niemeyer's 2003 Serpentine Pavilion – Brasília rendered petite. They also explain, but do not excuse, the pavilions by artists such as Jorge Pardo and architects like Jeanne Gang, which merely formalise technical and aesthetic inventions of more exploratory practices. That both projects have unfathomably yielded MacArthur prizes only serves as a reminder that the pavilion is in many ways emblematic of the proclivities of the art market and of technocratic instrumentalisation.

In its proliferation and professionalisation of all cultural services, pavilionisation is propelled forward by hyperpositivistic promises that each structure will provide ecological amelioration, social utility, structural efficiency and 'real' experience. These certainties derive from, but have also perverted, the 'real world' concerns of the 1970s into pseudoscience, hijacking (and thereby terminating) the potential of the pavilion as an experimental paradigm. The days of quixotic and experimental pavilions – Experiments in Art and Technology's Pepsi Pavilion at the 1970 Osaka Expo or Haus-Rucker-Co's Oase No 7 at Documenta 5 – that dreamed of offering immersive experience in utopian bubbles have been replaced by the more expansive and omnireaching model of projects such as Olafur Eliasson's, whose work has ranged from fans in small galleries, to solar flares across the global archipelago of Louis Vuitton store windows, to weather-altering devices inserted into existing spaces, to a series of works in which an entirely new structure has been built to produce the environment (*Your Rainbow Panorama*, 2006–11, or, with David Adjaye, *Your Black Horizon*, 2005). While the pavilion once generated interest as an interface between art and the world – most experimental pavilions of the 1970s were in fact predicated on a clear distinction between the two – interface is now the total surround. The difference between art and the actual world pivotal to Graham's reflections cannot obtain in an environmental paradigm filled with cultural diffractions, economic particulates and atmospheric variation.

Even though the pavilion as a production of a singular discipline or as an isolated object is no longer viable as either an interface between art and world or as an instantiation of the 'real' in this hybrid situation, its displacement from the privileged position of prolepsis has made new options available. The most important of these generate a complex interaction between art and architecture that produces objects, of which the pavilion might be one type, while shaping the complex and extensive networks in which these objects are situated. In other words, it is the intellectual project of the pavilion that negotiates between the life of the object as medium and form, and between the systems of organisation and discipline that link this object to others, which has potential today. For example, the photographs of Thomas Demand require both the construction and the demolition of pavilions – his paper models are full-scale, temporary architectural environments – but these pavilions are only one element in a system of interlocking paraworlds: adjacent and isomorphic productions, spaces and experiences that produce new forms of disciplinary interaction. Demand's preliminary images – models that appear in medias res – and final photographs do not occupy the same space, despite being spatial, nor do they add up to form a single work bound together by a traditional visual coherence or gestalt. Instead, each component can be read as a work and as a node, as an image and as an object, as an operation and as a thing.

The precise alchemy of these converging differences is intrinsically variable because it depends on how and if the viewer understands them to be linked, because some components circulate and others are site-specific, and because each element in the whole has a different lifespan as well as different mode of duration.

That Demand trained as a sculptor, works as a photographer, is an exceptionally keen student of architecture and eschews all such determinations, is itself a symptom of the variations in time and space that make his work a productive model for the contemporary. For *The Dailies* (2008–12), the twenty-fifth Kaldor Public Art Project in Sydney, Demand rejected all given display options. Instead, working like an architect, he toured the city to select his site, using an urban *dérive* as the first step in his design process. He chose a mid-century architectural oddity, a pavilion-scaled, circular eruption in the grid of downtown Sydney: a tiny hotel for a private club of ever-shrinking numbers of travelling salesmen, a modernist fossil in the shape of a ring of single rooms. In each of these rooms Demand hung a single photograph: his photos (smaller in scale than his typical works, placed in frames, and based on apparently casual iPhone shots taken on his travels through various parts of the world) were displayed as if native examples of hotel art. The hotel itself was treated as a natural habitat. The grooming behaviour of the cleaning staff was put into evidence, and invigilators were asked to remain in the hallway so that the visitor could 'happen upon' each room as if discovering an undisturbed waterhole. But these primitive huts were also repainted with high-quality wall paint, the cheap bedlinen was replaced with uniform spreads made of luxurious cloth, and the air mechanically spritzed with a bespoke Prada perfume. The net result was that each photograph in the space became attenuated across a network of increasingly diffuse atmospheres, behaviours, populations and objects. This even included a catalogue with concertina pages and a leporello binding, which, when open, approximated the shape of the building itself: a small

and portable post-pavilion with a vast butterfly effect
on its cultural ecology as a whole.

Like most butterflies, Demand's paper pavilions have
only an ephemeral presence, a delicacy totally at odds with
the serial monumentalisation of the pavilion that continues
unabated. If the exchange between art and architecture that
produced the conditions of possibility for the contemporary
pavilion began in the 'Rooms' of PS1, now MoMA's Young
Architects Programme and its many imitators are
hypertrophied symptoms of its conclusion. Having been
evacuated of every conceptual distinction, the pavilion is
reduced to a travesty of Krauss's 'sensuous immediacy' or
Graham's 'actual', mistaken for a naturally occurring site
of authentic experience or an actual environmental control,
but really just an opportunity for museums and other
commissioners to get 'real' architecture (and a fantastic
branding opportunity) at a steep discount. A regrettable
impact of this category error is that young architects
approach the pavilion as a stepping-stone to professional
practice rather than as an experimental project, even
though the construction of these pavilions is usually
woefully underfunded. Young architects are often forced to
spend their own money, exploit the labour of even younger
student architects, and then donate the models and
drawings produced along the way. Rather than being
without function or necessity, rather than being the means
to articulate an intellectual project, the pavilion has become
a first step in building a practice. Exploiting its capacity to
stage a 'reality effect' and its capacity to operate as a
building-as-manifesto, today's plastic parthenon makes
neither the future nor the present manifest. Instead, the
pavilion makes it really plain that once new architectural
ideas have been taken over by the now old desire for
professional achievement.

That Herzog & de Meuron and Ai Weiwei, two
unquestionable superproducers in our cultural landscape,
chose to entomb their 2012 Serpentine Pavilion, burying
half of their structure belowground and devoting much of
their effort to excavating the foundations of all previous

Serpentine pavilions, perhaps suggests that pavilionisation is approaching a state of self-referential exhaustion. Endings often do provoke such mourning, but this would be a better occasion for architects to recognise the need for inventing a new model of action, one not predicated on the difference between art and the world, but rather facing their profound imbrication. There is much to be gained from the cross-fertilisation between architecture and the arts that is enriching the contemporary cultural ecology, but the pavilion, now no more than a professionalised product without a project, has reached its limit.

First published in *Artforum*, October 2012

CONTEMPORARY

POP GOES THE BLACK BOX (2005)

The American roadside is one of the few places where
architecture has been permitted to go fast. Or at least
where the built vernacular has been permitted to go fast.
Architecture as a cultural practice – that is, the segment
of the field that not only selects and arranges but also
conceives and ideates – has typically been in favour of as
much permanence and stillness as it can muster. While a
few architects have made efforts to redeem the flickering
lights and rushing shapes of casinos, restaurants and
billboards, even the most ardent and self-proclaimed
advocate of vernacular and 'pop' architecture, Robert
Venturi, could only muster that this architecture of
fastness is 'almost all right'.[1]

John Lautner offers an even better example of the
architectural disdain for the quick pace imposed on
architecture by postwar commerce. Despite spending
most of his career in Los Angeles, the proverbial dumping
ground for all of America's quickly discarded cultural trash
– all the while enjoying the benefits of a practice funded
by the city's car and movie industries – despite being
considered the inventor of what is called the Googie style,
after one of the several car-oriented coffee shops he
designed, Lautner didn't come close to Venturi's sympathy
for the strip. He famously lamented that the Junkland of
southern California was made of nothing but 'fast food,
fast deals, fast everything'.[2]

Perhaps Lautner would have preferred the roadsides
of 1960s Italy, where the highways were venerated as
majestic engineering feats and speed was cultivated not
as a means to earn a quick buck but as an attribute of the
avant-garde. There he would have found Giovanni
Michelucci's Church of the Autostrada, one of the most

important examples of Italian organicism, a postwar architectural school directly rooted, like Lautner's own work, in the late work of Frank Lloyd Wright. The church pays no homage to the Alfa Romeos rushing by but instead mourns the death of workers killed during the highway's construction by turning concrete into an almost Whitmanesque poem.[3]

Wright's postwar work offered Lautner and Michelucci a perfectly ambivalent attitude towards the structure of the contemporary culture then developing around them. In a well-known example of this ambivalence, Wright cribbed the basic idea for the Guggenheim Museum from his own design for a parking structure – a structure required by the new pace of automotive life – but chose not to quicken the pace of architecture itself. Movement along the Guggenheim's spiral path is interrupted again and again by speed bumps that take the form of discrete niches in which individual works of art are hung. The museum's floor, its epistemological ground, appears to mobilise the viewer and is technically controlled by the mechanisms of speed, yet it causes a series of stops that produce the effect of slowing down. As much as they absorbed Wright's expressive concrete work, Lautner and Michelucci took over this simultaneous engagement with and denial of the multiplying forms of time that were altering the cultural landscape.

The net result was that Lautner's architecture was criticised for being too fast – Lautner-lovers still feel the need to protect him from the stain of Googies and an unseemly attachment to Hollywood – whereas Michelucci's church was faulted for being too slow – many critics found it overly monumental.

Lautner in Los Angeles and Michelucci in Milan both faced the same dilemma, related to the postwar period's polarisation of kitsch and the avant-garde into antithetical modes.[4] Generally understood in terms of high and low, the antithesis was also organised around radically different conceptions of time. Speed was conceived as heroic, masculine and advanced [5] – attributes that transformed it

into the prerogative of high modernist practice because
it promised to lead to a new form of monument. Marinetti
makes a classic demonstration of the link between speed
and monumentality in his manifesto on futurism. Speed
is used as a means to erase all traces of the nineteenth
century, allowing new forms of art and architecture to
emerge in their place. The urban and architectural schemes
Antonio Sant'Elia made in response – which were instantly
called dynamic forms – were thought to give the
appearance of swiftness to buildings and cities that were
themselves to be permanent. On the other hand, merely
going fast or speed without heroic monumentality was
considered to be kitsch and not only distinct from, but
aggressively debasing to, the values of high culture. Freud,
for example, argued that Americans had no patience for
psychoanalysis, their desire for a fast cure both undoing the
slow repeated conversations that constituted the praxis of
psychoanalysis and literally changing the structure of time
itself, such that 60 minutes could become the proverbial
analytic 50-minute hour. By the 1950s, surrounded by this
kind of mixed message – speed up but don't go fast –
architecture lost the ability to set the right cultural pace.

If Lautner and Michelucci both followed a single
road that began in Taliesin, their work ended up on a
transportation system with no clear beginning or end
and no single or dominant structure as a point of reference.
This metaphorical shift in the landscape of speed parallels
a more general change in architecture's relation to a
concurrent restructuring of cultural logic. In a classic essay
Reyner Banham argued that architectural modernism
had once had enough authority to produce and control
a coherent visual landscape,[6] and to hold in abeyance the
growing conflicts between mass consumption and
traditional aesthetic protocols. But between 1951 and 1961,
the discipline had lost its privileged cultural position as
master and measure of universal design values, first and
foremost because it had not learned to tell contemporary
time. Architects insisted on thinking in units of long
duration. Forty years was considered to be the minimum

desirable lifespan for a building, but almost all buildings were still conceived with the goal of lasting much longer. For Banham, 40 years was the threshold between fast enough and much too slow. Meanwhile, the designed landscape was operating in various shorter durations, including both brief phases of equilibrium – five to ten years – and small bursts of instant obsolescence – a single season.

Architecture hoped to find a way variously to keep up with or to impede the shifts in contemporary time by focusing on the roadside vernacular. Yet the buildings and theorisations of the strip were more a symptom than a cause of its developing sense of being out of sync. It was in fact engagement with another American export – television – that would ultimately sustain architecture's forward momentum. Although not so much a part of mainstream architectural discourse in the 1960s, the collision between architecture and this new medium would become the most important arena in which the implications of speed and time in postwar culture were played out. Lautner, for example, may not have addressed the architectural implications of television directly, in the same way that Frederick Kiesler wrote explicitly about the impact of radio. Nevertheless, his Chemosphere house has been celebrated as an example of architecture's response to television, for the way in which it transforms the picture window into TV screen and presents the view as a backdrop.[7] And indeed, a replica of the Chemosphere is now used as a TV studio.

The fundamentally perspectival link between architecture and TV required no deliberate analysis on Lautner's part because it fit so easily into the established conceptual framework linking architecture to the visual field. On the other hand, the implied transformation of the inhabitant into a perpetual TV watcher, fixed in place and always confronted by the same distant and idealised view, suggests the kind of misunderstanding of the episodic nature of postwar time that was harming architecture, in Banham's view. For some, TV was not just a domestic version of an increasingly familiar and familial screen, but an alien black box that was completely reshaping the ergonomics of domesticity, reconfiguring the urban landscape, and entering the flow of information delivery systems in such a way as to make communication of any kind difficult whatever the medium.

In a work called *Scomodo*, Bruno Munari, one of Italy's most important postwar artists and designers, powerfully captured the discomfort that arose from the clash of new and old media in even the most traditional domestic environments. A would-be newspaper reader seeks leisurely comfort on an over-stuffed chair that is unable to accommodate the unruly coupling of man and medium. Their conflict produces a series of jerky movements that can only be represented by a series of stop-motion photographs. This series of stills reflects the fact that by the late 1950s, industrial design, particularly in Italy, was rapidly stepping towards the epicentre of the new universe of speed. The first digital flip clock made its appearance around this time – one that was visually digital but in fact operated analogically. In part because design was precisely then emerging as a quasi-autonomous discipline forged out of the convergence of design history, industry and media, the field was best positioned to recognise that television was rapidly replacing architecture as the medium, even the environment, that would disseminate the new, variable and heterogeneous visual landscape to an increasingly sophisticated audience of visual consumers.

One of the leading figures of the Italian industrial design craze and a frequent collaborator of Munari was Achille Castiglioni, who originally trained as an architect

Achille and
Pier Giacomo Castiglioni,
Colori e Forme, 1957

but set up a design practice with his brothers.[8] In addition to scores of well-known objects, Castiglioni helped to shape the public perception of television in Italy. For the national broadcasting service, RAI, he designed a series of pavilions and exhibitions to communicate Italy's transformation from a fascist state that used radio technology to assert centralised power (what Heidegger called standing reserves) into a democratic state that understood its audience as cultural participants. Castiglioni worked for RAI even before Umberto Eco, the first semiologist to write directly about TV as a medium of communication, was hired to serve as its cultural editor.[9] Eco and Castiglioni shared the notion that TV was a creative medium, not merely in its production, but more importantly in its reception. According to Eco, repeated episodes of similar structure – for example the consistent format of the news – permitted viewers to gain confidence in the medium. At the same time the variable content of each episode – the news itself is not the same night after night – enabled unexpected interpretations to be interjected. Castiglioni's designed environments are themselves like a TV series, architectural episodes with a consistent format yet ephemeral content, creating a milieu of tremendous temporal elasticity.[10]

Castiglioni was not alone in designing either TV sets themselves or exhibits that considered the impact of this new technology on domestic design. But he was one of the first to take on TV as an instrument of cultural change independent from its characteristics as a physical object. Most importantly, he was one of the very few to use this structural engagement with media to initiate a feedback loop that would ultimately produce structures and environments that were physical and material but that used their architectural structure to produce synchronicity with, rather than interrupt, TV's role as a conceptual metronome for the pace of contemporary time. For example, in 1951 one of his first exhibitions for RAI was organised around an overhead, openwork frame that twisted upwards towards an illuminated ceiling. Along the fascia of the structure, the names of the days of the week appeared to be printed, but not always centred on the plane, sometimes even slipping off their beams, as if time itself could be altered by typographic error or poor graphic design. Recalling Tatlin's Monument to the Third International, Castiglioni drew the viewer into a temporal spiral, but rather than measure the world according to the stable and proportional tempo of the

Bolshevik revolution, the viewer's eye is twisted into time subsumed within a weekly TV schedule.

Castiglioni not only repeatedly returned to the notion that television was restructuring the calendar but exploited it as an architectural opportunity. If the 1951 exhibition considered how the days of week might become events on a television schedule, the previous year's exhibition focused on how the periodic visual spectacle of television would alter the cultural landscape, transforming it from a clearly hierarchical continuum of moments into a heterogeneous constellation of multifaceted images. The walls of the exhibition hall were animated by planes deployed like a futurist installation: a three-dimensional and linked series of seven geometrically complex display boards bearing abstract images as well as pictures of television personalities and programmes, moved dynamically across the room, announcing the first week of broadcasting of the Italian cultural channel. What Castiglioni called 'the culture of always' was fragmented, its bits embedded in an unfolding constellation wherein each star grabbed the attention of the 'man of today' for a brief moment of his orbit through the exhibition. By 1956, Castiglioni imagined movement both within and emanating from the television as he reconceived the apparatus as a large and interactive machine, a robotic toy manipulated by the visitor who uses the television image as mobile interface.

In 1960, the year of Lautner's Chemosphere, RAI moved its exhibition programme into the trade fair district of Milan, evidently to take advantage of a permanent building and site within the annual Fiera Milano, which would become a vital force in Italy's economic boom. But within two years, Castiglioni had subverted these stabilities by submitting them in turn to the logic of the episode. For roughly the next decade, the site and building served as a provisional armature for a series of reconfigurations. Year after year, Castiglioni's installation occupied the same footprint and site, but every other architectural feature was new. On the heels of a graffiti-covered concrete bunker, Castiglioni grew a totemic garden where TVs were embedded in a biomechanical environment filled with moving and still images. In 1965, he turned again to an almost-architecture; rather than a building, he constructed a simple open framework that was to be redesigned and constructed for every new TV season.

Two of Castiglioni's installations were instantly considered extraordinary. One was formed of a series of telescopic boxes of different lengths, each containing a

screen set at a different focal distance, the design dramatising the way TV transforms the viewer's sense of what is near and far. In the spirit of Eco, the most famous part of this exhibit was the unanticipated production of what the audience called the centipede, a creature with many legs formed by the viewers whose bodies were encased in the structure from the waist up. The slowly moving viewers

Achille and Pier Giacomo Castiglioni, RAI at the Milan Fair, 1965

collapsed into each other to become a new organism performing the watching of TV for others who, in turn, watched them watch. The following year revolved around the idea of TV characters. In a series of adaptations of classic Italian novels, the protagonists were played by actors who were already well known to Italian audiences as TV characters. These televised novels were broadcast

on small screens contained within enormously oversized cutouts of the characters suspended overhead, creating a supersandwich of fictional subjects: the character in the novel, the celebrity character, the TV character playing the literary character, etc. Exploding these various characters in search of an author, the exhibition produced a pre-Photoshop phantasmagoria of play-acting,

Achille and Pier Giacomo Castiglioni, RAI Pavilion at the Milan Fair, 1966

with still and moving TV images embedded into these gargantuan yet two-dimensional figures. The TVs set at eye level and the crowd of characters hanging from the ceiling were viewed not only at two different scales but in accordance with two different speeds. Although the visitor moved through the longitudinal space as if towards a conclusion, the contradiction between these various modes of addressing the viewer was never resolved. The installation terminated on an elevated platform that inserted the viewer into this mix of images at eye level, such that the disruptions to narrative pace and visual coherence introduced by the collision of television and the novel were not explained but rather exposed.

Castiglioni's fundamental interest lay in building the medium of TV, using space and structure to explore the mechanism of its apparatus, the way it regulates time, and its construction of narrative and character as primary components in a shifting landscape of communications. Castiglioni was of course not alone in having a general interest in TV, but his insistent association between not-quite-architectural but still physical experiments and the immaterial structures and mechanisms of TV is key to his specific understanding of the medium and its implications for contemporary culture. Indeed, the material dimension of his investigations grew increasingly in scale, tending more and more towards the radically environmental until 1968, when the project for RAI

Achille and Pier Giacomo Castiglioni, RAI Pavilion at the Milan Fair, 1968

culminated, perhaps even exploded. In the manner of the 'rotoliefs' Duchamp made for the anaemic cinema, Castiglioni created an auditory fantasy landscape of soundtracks of different shows going forwards and backwards, propelled by spinning disks. This installation was again placed within the same architectural structure used in previous years, but for the 1968 exhibition skin hung on the exterior did not reach the ground. Left exposed, this quasi-interior not only leaked its cacophony outwards, becoming an independent broadcasting apparatus, but was itself invaded by the city's ambient noise. The following year, in one of his final schemes for RAI, Castiglioni took a retrospective look at 15 years of Italian broadcasting with a pavilion interior formed out of TVs deployed as bricks, half in black and white and the other in the new world of colour. This architecture of information used the very pulse of the news, the drama of the ephemeral, to construct a building that conceived of its *durée* as 15 years of accumulated instants.

The historiography of architecture's response to the advent of TV has typically framed television as a domestic phenomenon that stabilised rituals of viewing and the normative cultural regimes these visual habits enforced, rather than the complex new temporalities TV introduced. But television culture was far from monolithic and the potential it offered to architecture was determined more by argument and interpretation than by factors intrinsic to the medium. For example, by the mid-1960s, the Castiglioni brothers would have been aware of the Eameses' well-publicised multiscreen installations, which took the TV out of the home and into the short-term environment of the World's Fair.[11] Yet the public screens made specifically for the fair were designed to mimic the bulbous aspect of the TV sets most Americans had at home. Not only did the shape of the screen establish continuity with the single-family homes in which the sets were imagined to be sitting, but each screen remained autonomous within the multiple, as if to remind the collective audience at the fair that the heroic authority of the individual was safe and sound at home. The Castiglioni pavilion of 1969, in contrast, emphasised TV's capacity to disrupt the individual as radically as it could disrupt time. In this way the scheme has less in common with the architecture of Lautner's Elrod House (also of 1969) than with the James Bond movie shot there – *Diamonds are Forever* – which itself is more like a TV series than a standalone film, with plots and characters that are both enduringly *sui generis* and completely interchangeable, repeatable and episodic.

In the midst of all this thinking about how to build the medium of television by exploring the device's capacity to simultaneously belong to the analogue and digital worlds and to seize upon the desynchronisation of these regimes for its architectural potential, Eco left RAI and Milan to become the professor of visual communications at the school of architecture in Florence. There he taught the students forming associations like Superstudio and Gruppo 9999, who by 1969 not only fully shared Eco's interest in mass culture and its technologies, particularly TV, but had also all been watching Castiglioni building TV for RAI for many years. Trained therefore to absorb the implications of new media on a structural level – rather than simply accommodating its intrusion into home design or imitating it as an aesthetic – these groups produced black box architecture: conceived through storyboarding rather than plans, sections and elevations, through materials that were simultaneously components and devices and understood not in the modernist terms of structure and other internal organs, but by its output and impact on the pulse of life in the world.

Black box architecture rendered obsolete the 'still-modernist' notion of a fast architecture sitting still on a roadside, where cars are allowed to speed but buildings must merely convey a sense of movement. Castiglioni himself felt that the RAI pavilions were too static, stuck as they were in Milan, and ultimately turned his attention to itinerant architecture that nomadically roamed around the countryside. Such an architecture was not needed to spread TV itself – TV was already everywhere – but had the explicit purpose of exposing viewers to the new logic of this medium, and to explain its impact on the built environment. When conceived as a means of cultural analysis rather than a technology to keep up with, TV made it possible to argue that the ephemeral was no longer the exception but was now the rule of architecture – not only in the obvious sense that things no longer lasted as long as they used to, but by breaking the traditional association of architectural value with durability and predictability. The strategies Castiglioni developed to build the medium of TV and to lay the foundation for black box architecture demonstrate that some ways of producing architecture engender more unpredictability than others, and that these ways are a matter of design rather than technology. In a powerful example of architecture that relinquishes the false promise of transparency for the obdurate effects of material shaped to have the greatest impact on the world, Castiglioni's entry to a 1940 competition for a local Fascist Party headquarters rejected the famous openwork grid of Giuseppe Terragni's Casa del Fascio in Como and

substituted instead a black box: two dense and impenetrable blocks of cheese are placed on a delicately sketched urban site plan, city building blocks that change shape as the cheese sags in the heat of the day, architecture that registers the passage of time but offers no clock face. These unadorned blocks, inexpressive and inert, riddled from within with irregular bubbles and pockets of spaces that ooze with utter unpredictability, are ironically timeless, yet and above all, are instantly consumable.

Achille Castiglioni, University Project, Casa del Fascio, 1939–40

NOTES

1. Robert Venturi and Denise Scott Brown are the architects best known for attempting to bridge the gap between what has been called architecture, the avant-garde, modernism and disciplinarity on the one hand; and the vernacular, the everyday and the unpedigreed on the other hand. Regarding his interest in the American roadside and the architecture of everyday commercial life, Venturi asked, 'Is not Main Street almost alright?' See Robert Venturi, *Complexity and Contradiction* (New York, NY: Museum of Modern Art, 1977).

2. 'Responsibility, Infinity, Nature', the transcript of a conversation between John Lautner and Marlene L Laskey (Oral History programme, University of Los Angeles, 1986)

contains countless scathing remarks about LA. See also Frank Escher, *John Lautner, Architect* (New York, NY: Princeton Architectural Press, 1998) and Nicholas Olsberg, ed, *Between Earth and Heaven: The Architecture of John Lautner* (New York, NY: Rizzoli, 2008).

3. Largely because of Bruno Zevi's interest in Frank Lloyd Wright, developed while Zevi was in the US during the Second World War, Italy was home to a significant neo-Wrightian revival. Zevi founded the association for Organic Architecture in 1944 and published *Verso un'architettura organica* (Turin: Einaudi, 1945). Like Lautner, Michelucci was a follower of Frank Lloyd Wright with a similar interest in rendering concrete as an organic building material. On Michelucci, see Claudia Conforti and Roberto Dulio, *Giovanni Michelucci 1881–1990* (Milan: Electa, 2007).

4. In this context, Clement Greenberg's classic essay 'Avant-Garde and Kitsch' in Partisan Review 6:5 (Fall 1939) and Gillo Dorfles et al, *Kitsch: The World of Bad Taste* (New York, NY: Universe Books, 1969) are most relevant.

5. For a rich discussion of the cultural history of speed, see the catalogue edited by Jeffrey T Schnapp, *Speed Limits* (Milan: Skira, 2009).

6. Banham's classic essay was reprinted as 'Banham, Reyner, "Design by Choice",' in Penny Sparke (ed), *Design by Choice* (London: Academy Editions, 1981), 97–107.

7. See for example Jon Yoder's dissertation, 'Sight Design: The Immersive Visuality of John Lautner' (Los Angeles: UCLA, 2010).

8. On Castiglioni's work, see Sergio Polano (ed), *Achille Castiglioni: Complete Works* (Milan: Electa, 2002).

9. While Eco's early role in the semiotics of popular culture and TV is well known, his role in the history of architecture and design has been given less attention, although there is now growing interest in the subject. On these matters see Giorgio Pigafetta, *Architettura moderna e ragione storica: la storiografia Italiana sull'architettura moderna, 1928–1976* (Milan: Guerini, 1993); Umberto Eco, *Appunti per una semiologia delle comunicazioni visive* (Milan: Bompiani, 1967) and 'Proposte per una Semiologia dell'Architettura', Marcatré, 1967, 34–36, 56–76; *Opera aperta* (Milan: Bompiani, 1962).

10. Much of the following discussion is based on a series of short articles and documents published in *Domus* on Castiglioni's RAI series. See 'Achille e Pier Giacomo Castiglioni: Il padiglioni Rai alla fiera de Milano', *Domus* 442 (1966), 32–35; 'Un padiglioni mobile per la RAI', *Domus* 455 (1967), 21–25 and 'Bianco e nero, alla Fiera de Milano' *Domus* 478 (1969), 19–21.

11. On the Eameses' multi-screen installations, see Beatriz Colomina, 'Enclosed by Images', in *Grey Room* 2 (Winter 2001), 26–29.

ANDY ARCHITECT™, OR, A FUNNY THING HAPPENED ON THE WAY TO THE DISCO (2008)

Andy Warhol was a fellow who knew his way around museums, so it comes as something of a surprise that he got lost on his way to one (maybe MoMA?) and found himself shopping instead. Or so he famously told an interviewer to preface his deadpan announcement that 'Bloomingdale's is my favourite museum'.[1] What is surprising about this displacement – from department store to museum – is not Warhol's preference itself, but rather that his remark constitutes a theory of architecture. Like much of Warhol's production, the statement appears somewhat banal at first glance, as if he was merely voicing the now common argument that shops look like museums and museums function as shops. His apparently offhand remark relies on the assumption that these typologies are, or should be, opposed to one another, and creates by association the amusing effect of a reversal of expectation. But even if reversed, these oppositions fail to displace the categories at hand, and it is in fact displacement that is at the root of Warhol's statement and its theoretical value for architecture. By using the superlative, 'my favourite', Warhol puts museums and department stores on a continuum in which categories such as typologies and programmes, and ultimately mediums and disciplines themselves, slip and slide across rather than oppose each other. This conceptual movement reorganises the cultural field to open a new space of possibility outside the confines established by the expected terms, even in unexpected combinations. So the profit in recalibrating the relationship between the avant-garde, typified by displays at MoMA, and kitsch, typified by sales at Bloomies, must be found neither in the museum nor in the department store but in another place, under the auspices of a certain Andy Warhol who, functioning as an architect – Andy Architect™ – produced a form of architecture that hasn't yet been named as such.

Of all the kinds of architectural kitsch that might make a museum shudder, the most offensive is no doubt disco, the butt of jokes by even the most ardent lovers of popular culture. But in 1967, as Hollywood was stealing the idea of the vulgar populus from ancient Rome in films such as *A Funny Thing Happened on the Way to the Forum*, Italy was packing up Andy Architect™ and taking him across the Atlantic to a disco. That year, a young Italian architect, Fabrizio Fiumi, came to New York on his second trip to the United States.[2] On the first, in 1964–65, Fiumi had arrived as a student of architecture in the grip of the Italian fascination with American organicism, dutifully eager to see the works of Frank Lloyd Wright.[3] By the second trip, Fiumi had been doubly radicalised: first by the British invasion, which led him to look out for Pink Floyd, and second by the exhibition 'Superarchitettura', held in Pistoia in 1966, which changed his attitude towards the possibilities pop culture offered to architecture. The exhibition was the first showing of what Germano Celant would later call 'Architettura Radicale', the manifesto for which began: 'Superarchitecture is the architecture of superproduction, of superconsumption, of the superinduction into consumerism, of the supermarket, of superman, and of the gasoline called Super.'[4] This combination led Fiumi not up to the Guggenheim, but down to the Electric Circus, the nightclub into which Warhol's Dom had been transformed, and where he collected the Velvet Underground, his films, various performers, hangers on and young architecture critics, and set them into motion as the Exploding Plastic Inevitable.[5]

The EPI is well known in the history of multi-media art, but understanding that it is also a signature project of Andy Architect™ reveals it to be not only art but also architecture radicalised as a medium.[6] Conceived in this way, the EPI constitutes an architectural design that used light and sound performance as materials to squeeze the empty space out of the existing room and refill it with a semi-solid environment. Cunningly isomorphic with traditional architectural space, the new interior used the exaggerated animations of its ambience to undo the legibility of the architectural frame. Indeed, the frame and the architectural apparatus from which it was constituted – the building, both its structure and its space – became irrelevant, a mere prop to the interior as such. One of the reasons the EPI is well known is because Marshall McLuhan used it as a model of his concept of allatonceness, which he saw as a regenerative and retribalising unity of mediums and experience. However, the architectural interpretation offers an alternative and perhaps more compelling reading. For McLuhan, the atmospheric indeterminacy created by the simultaneous deployment of multiple media tended towards a cohesive and immersive whole, but an architectural reading originates from a different understanding of the whole, one that does not begin or end with the media but instead embraces everything in the environment, including the architectural support system. From this perspective, it is possible to see that it was essential to EPI to have a gap between the ephemeral effects tending towards the allatonce and the spatial and structural envelopes that contained them and that tended towards clear systems of legibility. This gap generated a radically disjunctive experience that was not restorative but rather characterised by a barrage of simultaneous assaults that led to dissonance between types of experience and cognition. As the spectacle of media effects came to dominate the architecture, as minor and ephemeral effects came to overwhelm what should have been the major structure of the environment, viewers struggled to understand the experience. As one period reviewer of the EPI described it, 'the lights [are] a dim blue flicker that goes fast and slower … [but] just as your eyes get used to each kind of flicker… before your mind can grab it, it's become random and confusing again.'[7]

Perhaps Fiumi's double radicalisation had allowed his eyes to adjust to the increasingly stroboscopic present, making it possible for him, like others of his generation, to see this obscure and pulsing mass – otherwise resistant to traditional forms of architectural imageability – as the rupturous, rather than regenerative, solution to an emerging architectural critique of monumentality and power. Electrified by the experience of this architecture dangerously delaminated from its built container and constituted instead by a delirious atmosphere crowded with discontinuous bits of sound, light and flesh, Fiumi headed back to Italy. On the way, though, he stopped on Canal Street, where he bought a bundle of projectors that he carried to Leonardo Savioli, one of his professors at the University of Florence and a key figure in the education of virtually all of the 'Italian Radicals'.[8] Savioli then set the Electric Circus as the thesis topic for the year, turning Warhol into an architect, reoriginating media theories as an architectural brief, and replacing the museum, a traditional object of thesis study, with the disco or *Piper*, a place of fun and entertainment.[9] The goal of this exercise was nothing less than to use the disco as a means of reconfiguring allatonceness from a model of unity into a system of multiplication: proliferating the various strands of architectural research of the mid-60s; adding new media to the surface of architecture; substituting the collective social forms of popular and youth culture for traditional publics; and challenging architecture with the forms of duration and discontinuity developed in performance art, happenings and op art. Occasioning a total transformation of both the architectural medium and subject, as one of Savioli's student groups argued, the architecture of disco should be one 'of tactile audio and visual stimuli that implicate the operator in an active … participation … [T]he spectator will become an actor in a space undergoing continual transformation in which luminous effects create a total disorientation in the universe of Cartesian geometry.'[10]

The student projects in this thesis course vary, but only within certain parameters. All take architecture slumming by downgrading its constituent elements: machines become gadgets, symbols become coke bottles and details become decultured. Yet along with this semiotic downward spiral came an upsurge in special effects produced by every conceivable type of media.

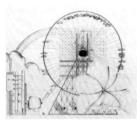

Human traffic is mechanised and choreographed to increase congestion and crowding; surfaces are polished to produce excessive reflexivity; space frames create constant noise in the visual field; automobiles and parking become occasions for spectacle; and projected images and soundtracks both amplify the environments

Alessandro Poli, Piper Club, c1966

but more importantly structure them, replacing traditional architectural markers like walls, floors or even volumes. As media usurp and in so doing transform traditional architectural functions like articulating space and organising experience, they also begin to infiltrate architectural means of representation.

Although most students used or implied the use of media in their designs, they all produced physical models and drawings. The use of these conventional representational categories makes visible the radical nature of *how* they were used, both in relation to individual objects and as a palette of possible representational operations. For example, virtually all the models are roughly assembled concatenations of primarily found mechanical objects. Their principal collective attribute is inexactness, as if they bore no responsibility to model or represent a project in its details. In fact, the models suggest that the architecture of these projects, like the EPI, is fundamentally unknowable. On the other hand, the students also produced precisely measured drawings, Beaux-Arts in both scale and finish. These drawings not only describe specific projects in exacting detail, but function precisely as academic demonstrations of architectural knowledge itself.[11] Every project is thus internally divided between media effects of

99

impenetrable allatonceness ironically shaped by physical models, and the representation of 'real' architecture made visible only in the virtual environment of the drawings. The models that aspire to the overwhelming spectacle of media and the drawings that seek to concretise architectural intellection never coincide adequately and therefore leave architecture exposed to an epistemological paradox.

It was precisely through these wildly divergent representations that Fiumi and his thesis group realised the most radical potentials of the collision they had orchestrated between architecture and new media. Their project powerfully exploited this misalignment between the flat drawing as plane of representation and the three-dimensional model as space of action to explore how architecture could go beyond merely offering its surfaces as backdrop for the application of media images, and could actually produce media effects. Plans drawn on transparent paper were superimposed and placed over a neon light to generate a three-dimensional drawing. On the one hand,

Caveada, Fiumi, Galli and Lorenzi, Piper Club, 1966/67

the illuminated drawing mimics the appearance of an image on a screen, particularly a TV screen. But more transformative than this visual analogy is the fact that the drawing thickens into something more than a flat plane, into something model-like by virtue of being made of several layers of paper in its ideal viewing state. The three-dimensional image produced by the overlay also has the spatialising perceptual effect of an axonometric. Finally, because it has an on and off switch and the deep image is visible only episodically, the drawing performs like an apparatus from which the representation emanates. The ideation of architecture is itself televisual and intermittent.

Through these exploding inevitables, Warhol became Andy Architect™, and disco a new architectural diagram. Every project in Savioli's studio pursued allatonceness to disrupt normal systems of architectural coherence by conceiving of the superimposition of new media on both buildings and the representations that produce them as a material layer added to the architectural medium. Indeed, if architectural conventions were abandoned to accommodate systems of allatonceness, the lightning speed with which McLuhan's ideas were taken up suggests not a loss for architecture or its dematerialisation but rather a dimensional gain and an expansion of the representational strategies that could generate specifically architectural operations. Allatonceness immediately invited exploration by architecture because the idea was already architectural.[12] Ironically, then, while McLuhan had for example used architecture and spatial descriptors to explain an idea purportedly about TV and how it was going to put an end to things like architecture – a key image in McLuhan's analysis is children at home sitting too close to the TV set – he failed to grasp the true significance of his ideas for the field of architecture. The more his metaphorically architectural notion of allatonceness came into contact with emerging spatial mediums such as the EPI, and the more allatonceness was reoriginated in architecture, the more the familiar refrain of 'this will kill that' was exposed as an empty threat.

McLuhan's understanding of the space of television was predicated on the scale of the domestic environment: the proximity to the TV set that was guaranteed by the size of a typical house is the unstated precondition for McLuhan's notion that TV is immersive. But architecture as a field knew better than to rely on the conventions of domestic containment to find its way into the logic of new media. For example, in a sublime example of historical allatonceness, in 1967 – the year of McLuhan's *Medium is the Message* and the year of the superarchitecture *Pipers* – a spate of articles appeared in architectural journals describing the reappropriation of projective devices from stage and display windows for private uses, often citing both the Electric Circus and McLuhan's theory of allatonceness.[13] The results, called instant interiors and turned-on décors, were characterised by spatial totality – in which floors, ceilings and walls were charged with 'high fantasy' images – and by instantaneousness as events, by décors understood not as ornament but in terms of the capacity to suddenly appear and disappear. Constantly shifting and intermittent projections spilled promiscuously into these spaces, flickering on top of human figures and through transparent furniture until, in a surreal topological inversion, the entire interior, instead of containing a TV set, became TV itself. Generating luminous and flickering ambience, the superarchitecture of the superephemeral removed architecture from the logic of inside and out, public and private, and even from the coordinates that distinguish walls from floors, up from down, plans from sections. The plastic medium of architecture was exploded, becoming a supermedium that overlaid and superimposed on architecture's propensity to stabilise images and form the radically disruptive capacity of the instant. Allatonceness was not putting an end to architecture: architecture used allatonceness to generate a theory of the just once: just once and just once again.

By 1968, so-called turned-on décor was again on the move and had become the instant exterior. In that year, Washington DC was lit up by an 'electric environment' strategically turned on by Doug Michels, before he became part of Ant Farm, on the same evening that traditional urban beautifiers were meeting to discuss how to develop the Georgetown waterfront.[14] Like all good students of architecture during the 1960s, Michels really wanted to be in a band. The architectural collective was the closest alternative for those who didn't play guitar. Fiumi, too, had formed Gruppo 9999 and staged a series of architectural happenings all over Florence modelled as much on the Rolling Stones as on the Living Theatre.[15] By using flashing strobe lights, music, television, passersby and performers as constituent elements, architecture became a supermedium characterised by the exaggeration of ambient effects, the delamination of architectural experience from the technical support of building, and the thickening of the architectural surface with the superimposition of new layers of mediatised matter. This was where the EPI had taken architecture in only two years: disco had become an abstract diagram of a new theory of the discipline, and its effects were themselves electric.

Shortly after the Savioli thesis concluded, Pipers and the episodic architecture they generated started a sweep up and down the boot of Italy, transforming a series of once relatively autonomous architectural centres into a coherent design landscape, a kind of disco-age reprise of Garibaldi's unification of the nation's states in the nineteenth century. From Rome to Rimini, Pipers became not only venues where an emerging generation was entrained to function as a new architectural audience able to manoeuvre through allatonceness, but also galleries showing both real and ersatz contemporary art, fashion and the burgeoning productions of industrial design. In Turin, an impending Piper generated so much interest that the client abandoned the project in fear of mobs suffering from disco fever. As a result the architect, Pietro Derossi, founding member of Gruppo Strum, became both architect and entrepreneur, using a time-sharing scheme to support the club.[16] Music and dance on Friday and Saturday evenings geared towards the Fiat factory labour force (the ideal public of the Italian left) supported weekday functioning as a contemporary art gallery and performance space: when the Living Theatre was shut down in New York, it came to

Gruppo 9999, Space Electronic, Florence, 1969

the Turin Piper. The two regimes colluded in the production of the club's décor, where factory workers dancing amid an artwork of projected human figures in the style of Warhol's Superstars created a constant swell of bodies across lines of temporality and class. The Bang Bang club opened the following year in Milan, linked via an acrylic elevator chute to a clothing store designed by the intermedia architect Ugo La Pietra. Just then, Gruppo 9999 were finishing Space Electronic in Florence, where shiny aluminium on the floor reflected the movements of a large parachute (also carried by Fiumi from the US) that was suspended like a droopy piece of film, or a superhero's cape, from the ceiling.[17] Gruppo 9999 (pronounced 99:99 like the hypothetical moment on a digital clock just before lift-off) described their spatial goals in this architecture of overhead projectors, films, slides, stage lights, live performances, recorded music, theatre and happenings, as evanescent, mobile and fluttering. They asked, 'Why do we think that space is not made by sounds and perfumes or by the dark?' [18] Even if they were ephemeral and instantaneous, utterly dependent on the activation of media technologies for their effects, the atmospheric elasticity and durational instability of the materials used by these disco architects permitted illusive yet identifiably architectural environments to emerge.

The march of the Pipers came to an end as Derossi opened L'Altro Mondo in Rimini, a disco that received substantive critical attention. According to Peter Cook,

Pietro Derossi, Altro Mondo Club, Rimini, 1967

it was the only contemporary Italian work to have overcome Italy's 'unfortunate national propensity for abstract philosophy' and 'hypersensitivity to serious values' and to have understood that a 'definably new architecture' would unfold along with and through the user and be generated not from hardware but from 'the moment' and its atmospherics.[19] *Domus* described the club as an 'electrically extended architecture' best considered a field of 'now and then'.[20]

These events – instant interiors and exteriors – belong to the widespread use of projection technologies in the 1960s across many disciplines, but they also expose the specific parameters that emerged as the instantaneous and the projected image became an architectural and urban system. By the mid-60s architecture was abandoning the system of expanded cinema, exemplified by the work of

Frederick Kiesler and the Eameses, and resisting the understanding of walls as merely extra-large screens bearing images without intrinsic matter or consequence. Instead, architec-ture increasingly exploited the effects of direct contact between image and the architectural surface

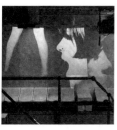

Pietro Derossi,
Piper Club, Turin, 1966

and between virtual image and moving bodies, using projections as an added layer of matter and as extensions of the architectural medium and eventhood. Architecture was now not simply the accommodator of TV sets or film screens or subject to the dematerialising force of projected images. Instead, in surfaces thickened with moving images and illuminated bodies, spaces filled up

with undulat-ing waves of sound and light, and in representational techniques poised between the flatness of drawing and the animated three-dimensionality of digital media, the discipline found the means to become an exploded supermedium.

Faint after-images of the stroboscopic Pipers were to be seen in Emilio Ambasz's 1972 exhibition *Italy: The New Domestic Landscape*. Many designers included in the MoMA show had been students in Savioli's course, and all of the Piper architects – Pietro Derossi, Ugo La Pietra and Gruppo 9999 – were featured. But the images are only faint because the exhibition resisted the ambiguities of the architecture of now and then with an overcompensating effort to classify. The show had a dizzyingly extensive taxonomy – objects selected for their formal and technical means, objects selected for their sociocultural implications, design as postulation, design as commentary, counterdesign as postulation – that vainly attempted to fix objects and ambitions that were formulated precisely in order to be promiscuously mobile with respect to both medium and audience. The only escape from this category compulsion was incidental: each installation set on a black box stage was obliged to use television in place of wall text, such that the principal source of continuity in this landscape was less the rites of domesticity as intended by Ambasz than the ambient effects of soundstage leakage: the flickering luminosity of the cathode ray and the overlapping noises of simultaneous TV loops.

If the taxonomic interest of museum culture underestimated architecture's capacity to move beyond such normative positions as pro or con, avant-garde and kitsch, the Piper phenomenon resonates more loudly with a return to Andy Architect™, with his declassifying love of Bloomingdale's, and to the impossible to classify places this love created – EPI, obviously, as well as the Factory (which was workplace, event space, store, gallery, installation and home). Even a tiny, short-lived disco in Turin was an equally fictitious and materially monolithic showroom that didn't sell anything, a gallery where the objects could be used, an intimate environment where no one lived but where an emerging generation was always at home. From such rather dubious vantage points it becomes possible to find other Piper phenomena and the effects of their reformulation of the architectural medium in surprisingly legitimate places. *Architectural Record* of 1978 selected none other than Studio 54 as a Record Interior of the year, surely a form of Andy Architecture™.[21] This ultimate disco rendered space and experience as completely detached from the logic of building and produced instead by atmospherics-yielding stages, on which the primary architectural event gets turned off and on under a flickering spotlight that multiplies the once unique and ideal observer into an endless series of performers and superstars. Architects had to invent the idea of Andy Architect™ in order to get architecture to go beyond the fixed formal economies of both the avant-garde and kitsch.[22] In turn Warhol, who literally made an art of cribbing from his own imitators, ultimately used the radically displaced notion of architecture he had induced in others as model for his own work: referring to *Shadows*, the series of 102 paintings also made in 1978, Warhol quipped that they were not art, but disco décor.[23] And today's disco fever demonstrates that

Andy Architect™ has not yet finished playing.[24] Indeed, a new generation of would-be radicals, who evince an interest in theories of imageability that confound traditional notions of architectural duration by deploying promiscuous, semi-solid forms and materials along with spectacular surface effects, will find useful if fantastically suspect alibis in those always discounted by architectural history as mere dancing queens.

First published in *Log* 15 (2009)

NOTES

1. Like most of Warhol's aphorisms, there are many versions of this comment, which was repeated in endless contexts. For one, see the interview with Tracy Brobston, 'A Shopping Spree in Bloomingdale's with Andy Warhol', reprinted in Kenneth Goldsmith (ed), *I'll Be Your Mirror: The Selected Andy Warhol Interviews* (New York, NY: Carroll & Graf, 2004), 301–II.

2. Author interview with Fiumi (Venice, CA, 27 December 2006).

3. Italian architectural culture of the early 1960s was still largely dominated by Bruno Zevi, whose first book, *Verso un'architettura organica*, appeared in 1945. Zevi had had an epiphanic visit with Frank Lloyd Wright while he was in exile in the US during the Second World War.

4. 'La superarchitettura e l'architettura della superproduzione, del superconsumo, della superinduzione al consumo, del supermarket, del superman e della benzina super. La superarchitettura accetta la logica della produzione e del consumo e vi esercita un'azione demistificante.' My translation from the manifesto for the I966 exhibition 'Superarchitettura', which took place in Pistoia. The poster is reproduced in Lara-Vinca Masini, *L'Arte del Novecento: dall'espressionismo al multimedia* (Florence: L'Espresso, 2003), 989. 'Superarchitettura II' took place in the Galleria Communale, Modena, 1967.

5. The EPI first took place inside and was distinct from the 'Dom' on St Mark's Place in I966. The Dom was itself an informal renovation of a collection of social spaces and clubs that had grown together piecemeal over time. By 1967 the club's ownership was transferred and renamed the Electric Circus. Charles Gwathmey, who had just incorporated his firm as Gwathmey, Henderson and Siegel, Architects, redesigned the club in 1969 – a formalisation of the once ad hoc space that has been associated with its decreasing popularity. *Progressive Architecture* described the renovation as overly fixed and permanent: 'in spite of lasers slicing through space, slides flashing on all

surfaces, and music pulsing every atom, the tactility quotient of space defined by such formal perfection is zero. [L]oose music in an uptight room.' See *P/A News Report* 34 (June 1969). The club closed in 1971. Herbert Muschamp often described how he frequently operated the projectors for the EPI.

6. For an important reading of the EPI from the perspective of Warhol's oeuvre and the development of media-art, see Branden W Joseph, 'My Mind Split Open: Andy Warhol's Exploding Plastic Inevitable', *Grey Room* 8 (Summer 2002), 80–107.

7. Larry McCombs, 'Chicago Happenings', *Boston Broadside*, July 1966, in 'Scrapbook' v 2 Small, 7, Warhol Archives. Cited in Joseph, 97.

8. On Savioli, see the exhibition catalogue *Leonardo Savioli grafico e architetto* (Florence: CentroDi, 1982). The term 'radical architecture', as applied to Superstudio, Archizoom and other Italian groups, was coined by Germano Celant in his catalogue essay for *The New Italian Landscape* (New York, NY: Museum of Modern Art, 1972). See also Celant's *The Italian Metamorphosis 1943– 1968*, with a foreword by Umberto Eco (New York, NY: Guggenheim Publications, 1994).

9. Some of the student work done for Savioli is documented in his *Ipotesi di Spazio*, Florence, 1972.

10. The name of the assigned theme of the academic year 1966–67 was 'Il Piper, Architettura di luce e movimento' (Piper, Architecture of light and movement.) A group composed of students Breschi, Cecchini, Cini, Curcian and Fiorenzoli, described their particular project as follows: 'Facciamo un'architettura de stimuli tattili-audio-visivi, che inseriscono il fuitore in una partecipazione attiva-creative … Lo spettatore diventa attore in uno spazio in continua trasformazione, di cui l'effetto luminoso ne è un interprete importantissimo e riesca a creare un disorientamento totale nell'universo Cartesiano geometrizzato.' See Savioli, *Ipotesi*, 29, my translation.

11. Sandro Poli, who would later join Superstudio and design *Interplanetary Architecture* – one of Superstudio's best known multimedia projects that included drawings, collages, films and storyboards, amongst other things – described in a 2006 interview with the author how he copied/borrowed parts of Archigram projects in his drawings and that such work, so well known to students, was still totally unknown to the senior faculty. The appropriation went unnoticed by the jury, much to the naughty pleasure of the students.

12. Umberto Eco, as professor of Visual Communication at the University of Florence from 1965–69, would have primed students at the school of architecture to think about architecture in mediatised terms and to be astute readers of McLuhan, whose *The Gutenberg Galaxy, Understanding Media* and *The Medium is the Massage* were all reviewed by *Domus* in 1967.

13. See 'Instant Interiors', *Progressive Architecture* 48:6 (June 1967), 176–81 and 'Projection: The New Turned-On Décor', *House Beautiful* 109:9 (1967), 130–32. One project described in House Beautiful was the apartment of C Ray Smith, author of *Supermannerism: New Attitudes in Post-Modern Architecture* (New York, NY: Dutton, 1977). The best-known apologia and theoretically most disdained treatment of early postmodernism, the book includes

extended discussions of the formal attributes of disco design culture, the impact of McLuhan and the Electric Circus in particular.

14. See 'Instant Exteriors', *Progressive Architecture*, March 1968.

15. The group's work of this period, and particularly their performance pieces, is best documented in a self-published, limited edition book, *Ricordi di Architettura* (Florence, 1972). The group had no particular leader and its members included M Preti, P Coggiola, A Gigli, C Caldini, G Sani and P Galli. Fiumi, who died in 2013, became a film editor. The group's name varies from publication to publication and for the 1968 Happening they called themselves 1999. Galli, in a 2006 interview with the author, clarified that the final name became Gruppo 9999. On the significance of the name, see below.

16. Author interview with Derossi, October 2006. On Derossi, see his *Per un'architettura narrativa; Architetture e progetti 1959–2000* (Milan: Skira 2000).

17. See Gruppo 9999, *Ricordi di Architettura* (Florence, 1972). I'd like to thank Galli, Stella Targetti and Pino Brugellis for their kind assistance in acquiring access to this material.

18. *Ricordi di Architettura*, 101.

19. Peter Cook, *Experimental Architecture* (New York, NY: Universe Books, 1970), 83–84, 141.

20. See Tommaso Trini, 'Divertimentifici', *Domus* 458 (January 1968).

21. Paul Rudolph's New York apartment and Gwathmey Siegel's designs for Vidal Sassoon hair salons were other interiors recognised by *Record* and are further discussed in this volume in the essay Supercharged.

22. Ben van Berkel has written about his interest in Warhol as a model for developing a new kind of cultural economy for architecture. See his essay 'After Image', in *UN Studio: Design Models, Architecture, Urbanism, Infrastructure* (London: Thames & Hudson, 2006).

23. Andy Warhol, 'Painter Hangs His Own Paintings', *New York Magazine*, 5 February 1979.

24. A wide range of architects and artists, from Frank Gehry to Herzog & de Meuron, Olafur Eliasson, Office d/A, Greg Lynn and Foreign Office Architects have explored the effects of faceted, reflective silverised surfaces. In fact, disco décor may be one of the few common denominators of contemporary architectural design.

POOF (2006)

'There was a desert wind blowing that night. It was one of those hot Santa Ana's that come down through the mountain passes and curl your hair and make your nerves jump and your skin itch. On nights like that... meek little wives feel the edge of the carving knife and study their husband's necks. Anything can happen.'[1] The iconic opening to Raymond Chandler's *Red Wind* captures the volatility of a weather anomaly peculiar to Southern California, when arid and gusty airflows blow from the desert and mountains down toward the coast. The hot air currents moving quixotically at high speeds are notorious for fanning seasonal wildfires, and so are known, not just as the Santa Anas, but as the 'Devil's Breath' or 'Murder Winds'.

Another kind of unexpected conflagration caused by too much air and heat blowing around Orange County took place in 1969, when an enormous balloon – a mockup and material test for the famous Pepsi Pavilion built for the 1970 Osaka Expo – blew up in the desert. The pavilion started out quite prosaically. Pepsi Japan's first idea had been to host a rock competition in a simple band shell, a scheme that began to unravel when the Beatles refused to come and the shell turned out to have unacceptable acoustics. With the rock and roll programming diminishing in importance, the physical environment of the pavilion became an increasingly determining factor in the company's thinking. Discothèques, light shows and the Electric Circus were discussed as possible models for making a pavilion that would attract young people.

It was at this point in the discussion that Experiments in Art and Technology (EAT), the collective established by engineer Billy Klüver, got involved.[2] EAT decided to emphasise the production of experience as such, though they did not entirely leave behind the world of the music club – one initial inspiration came from the fantasy of peeping up a go-go dancer's skirt.[3] The mirror had been a fixture of nightclubs worldwide since the 1920s, when Art Deco design used faceted mirrors to enhance the glamour and mystique of night-time lighting effects. By 1968, mirror effects and rock and roll came together in clubs like Whiskey-a-go-go, where dancing girls were placed on elevated platforms with transparent bottoms and domed mirrored tops: looking up, club-goers would see the dancer doubled – as if dancing with herself upside down. EAT's innovation was to expand this seductive experience. Designing the interior space of their pavilion, they imagined the mirror unfurled and draped around the crowd like an enveloping curtain that extended through its curvature to visual completeness – a universe without limiting edges, entrancing all vision into peripherality. Through this fully spherical mirror, the particular programme of dancers and discos, as well as the iconography of PepsiCo, was transfigured into a radically new type of environment.

EAT's stated goal was to critique what they called the gimmicky hysteria and excessive regimentation of world expos by providing visitors with an abstract, entirely self-directed and unscripted experience. Paradoxically, however, much of EAT's effort was devoted to precisely engineering the container of this amorphous sensation. A series of material trials for what EAT called the mirror dome were made, including two 20ft models constructed at the MGM studios in Culver City. As these exercises neither mastered the necessary technical precision nor provided persuasively experiential facsimiles, EAT opted to build a full-scale mock-up. Ironically, the only structure big enough to accommodate this radical experiment in support of the freedom of experience was a part of Eisenhower's military industrial complex, specifically a blimp hangar at the Marine Corps Air Station in Santa Ana. EAT's structure was a massive inflatable, 90ft in diameter and 55ft high, made of 13,000 square feet of mirrorised Mylar one thousandth of an inch thick, divided into 64 elliptical

EXTREME CLOSEUP OF POINT WHERE
EXPLOSION OCCURRED

EAT R+D Mirror Dome,
Santa Ana, 1969

sections to give a surface that was geometrically true to within a few millionths of an inch. All this engineering created a shimmering silver universe, a virtual world of hovering reflections. More prosaically, it also produced a tensile structure under too much air pressure which, after 12 spectacular minutes in September 1969, disappeared in an equally spectacular explosion.

The failure of the Santa Ana mirror dome was a kind of architectural Big Bang, registering the impact of a seismic shift in categorical tectonics and intellectual currents, and marking the beginning of a tremendous expansion of architecture's purview. When EAT filled the void space of their pure geometry with the particulars and particulates of Santa Ana Winds, when the stuff of their structure quite literally became regional and specific rather than abstract and utopian, architecture did not find the spirit of Orange County but rather was exploded by the global animations of environment and atmosphere. While the mirror dome took shape in southern California, testing for the structure was nomadic, taking place in various spots in California, South Dakota, New York and Japan. Klüver himself was a Swede who worked for Bell Labs in New Jersey. EAT's scheme was of course to be constructed in Japan, with the purpose of inculcating Asian youngsters into an American-style youth culture: PepsiCo's hope seems to have been that after entering the dome and inhaling its bubbly aroma, this transnational youth would drift off into a global diaspora of Pepsi-drinkers.

The Pepsi Pavilion subsumed the clarity of architectural space and the identity of place into a complexly dynamic and shifting environmental logic. This transformation parallels the shifts that took place in the roles played by the various producers of the pavilion and in the ways they understood that it would be received. For example, after much negotiation and debate between EAT and PepsiCo on the appropriate level of corporate presence in the pavilion, visitors could not get even a single sip of Pepsi to drink once they were inside. Similarly, after many efforts to redesign the Pepsi logo into something more abstract, less visible and more in keeping with the overall aesthetic environment they had in mind, EAT managed to convince the company to allow them to construct the pavilion without a single logo anywhere.[4] Of course, the net result of these victories of art over commerce was that the pavilion itself became a logo – a vehicle to provide PepsiCo with a new brand identity. So while PepsiCo planned to extend the run of their advertising campaign by transporting the pavilion throughout Japan, Klüver considered it 'the largest single most complex and difficult work of art produced in our time', one not to be 'used in any other context, commercialised or reproduced'.[5] In other words, while EAT did not consider itself an art organisation, its members saw the pavilion as a work of art and Pepsi as a patron. On the other hand, for David Thomas, vice-president in charge of marketing and distribution, the pavilion was a mobile, architectural-scale marketing campaign smartly disguised as a piece of contemporary art.

Gene Youngblood, a Los Angeles-based media critic, went to Santa Ana and saw the Mylar mock-up. He wrote, 'the effect is utterly indescribable. One is overwhelmed … [as] phantasmagorias of colour and light whirl … insanely about the environment. But "environment" is inadequate to describe this experience of place. It's there and it's not there.'[6] Youngblood's inability to grasp its structure reflects the fact that ownership, copyright, medium, location and duration – amongst other epistemological categories – were all put in question, even already at the mock-up stage. By the time the final project was built in Osaka, the effects of the Santa Ana mirror were multiplied ad infinitum. There, it was triple-shelled: the mirror was put in a quasi-geodesic dome (one military casement succeeding another, and moreover a known architectural type), which was in turn shrouded in a fog sculpture. While the faceted dome was the architectural point of departure and the very structure of the pavilion, the mirror and the fog were conceived from the outset as means of making this structure disappear. Like the great triple-shelled domes of the seventeenth century – designed to satisfy what were considered to be the different visual responsibilities of a dome to the outside and to the interior, but to do so in the service of creating an overall effect of visual infinitude – the pavilion's scheme was rooted in a clear division of surface, structure and atmosphere. But this division and the structural precision on which it relied was cloaked to give the overall object the same optical amorphousness in the interior as the atmospheric amorphousness on the exterior.

The calculated engineering of formlessness continued in the design of visitor experience. Stewardesses in mod outfits guided visitors through a tunnel that led to a below-ground unlit space where each person was given a handset as the first step in what EAT considered to be their transformation from beholder or customer into participant. As visitors moved up into the main space, where the floor was divided into seven sections, each made of different materials corresponding to particular pieces of pre-recorded sound, the hand units interacted with ambient noise as well as surround-sound that worked through 37 speakers and coils in the floor. The whole system, which included computerised sound, lighting and live performances, relied on the mobility of the visitor to trigger

EAT Pepsi Dome Interior, Osaka, 1970

feedback, creating an auditory hallucination equivalent to the optical effects. There was nothing particular to do, no circulation path to follow inside the dome, but as visitors milled around they both had, and made for others, an experience in which multiple sources of visual and auditory stimulation created an intense but unfocused, kinaesthetic, and always shifting environment. And so while the programming of the sound effects and performances changed every week over the course of the

expo – in contrast to the fixed nature of most fair exhibits –
it was also in flux moment to moment because each visitor
not only 'composed their own experience' but in so doing
altered in real time the experience of their fellow
participants.[7]

The interaction between all the components –
structural and material, atmospheric and environmental –
makes the whole best understood as a single, massive,
cybernetically controlled artificial organism. Yet the
pavilion is well known for only the software part of this
equation; while it is a canonic monument in intermedia
and performance studies, it remains almost entirely
unknown from an architectural point of view. This neglect
is surprising, considering how much credit Klüver gave
to the project architect. According to a description of one
of EAT's internal meetings, 'Billy said to the group in his
fiercest manner, "You guys have had it. You've talked long
enough".' Without the guidance of an architect, Klüver
complained, the collaboration consisted only of so much
hot air. At that point, he took matters into his own hands
by bringing in a project architect, who brought 'a totally
new reality' to the collaboration and who, according to the
art critic Barbara Rose, became the glue of the entire effort.[8]
The resulting transformation was profound: 'the project
changed from a free-for-all to something directed.' This
project architect was none other than John Pearce, who
had received a BArch from Yale in 1965. He studied with
visiting professor Ulrich Franzen, but after graduating
elected to work for Paul Rudolph instead since he considered
him the more creative of the two. Joining the Pepsi project
in November 1968 was Pearce's first independent job
post-Rudolph, aside from a brief stint working for Davis
Brody on the US pavilion. He was no stranger to the design
of exuberant and extravagant surfaces, having been placed
in charge of the renovation of Rudolph's own apartment in
1966, with a particular responsibility for the Plexiglas
components that were a major feature of its interior design.
The unprecedented scale and form of the Osaka pavilion,
however, offered Pearce the opportunity to explore how the

intrusion into architecture of yet another recently devised material that clung to surfaces, and hence did not behave in accordance with traditional tectonic logic, could generate a whole new range of atmospheric effects.

Pearce's involvement in the project, although clarifying the process and essential to the scheme's realisation, only accentuates the contradictory nature of the pavilion from an analytic perspective. Even as Klüver credited him with saving the project from degenerating into a 'free-for-all', Pearce was pointing out that no member of EAT considered the pavilion an architectural project, stating that 'these guys didn't even seem to realise that they were really building a building'.[9] Nor did he seem to think much of

EAT Pepsi Pavilion first model, 1969

the building as such either, describing his own function as being to free the artists by making the toilets disappear. Somehow, then, not even the conventional apparatus of a building – an entry, functional spaces such as offices and snack bars – and not even

a licensed architect with an Ivy League degree could make the pavilion visible as architecture. But it was not clearly recognisable as an art object either. Robert Rauschenberg, a member of EAT at the time, called the pavilion an invisible environment, because it was produced as a whole, beyond individually distinct and autonomous objects, by artists working outside their specific medium. Both Youngblood and Rauschenberg found the pavilion perceptually difficult, but it was in fact hard not to see – on the contrary, every available account describes the experience of the pavilion as an oversaturated spectacle. Instead, the difficulty derived from the fact that it did not present itself within recognisable disciplinary paradigms. Everyone could see the pavilion, but no one had the means to receive this new type of environmental intoxicant.

Another of Youngblood's remarks underscores the pavilion's resistance to those systems of visibility then prevailing even at the edge of the dictates of conventional visual culture. He described the dome as 'an astonishing, spectacular, radiantly sensuous, transcendentally surrealistic giant mirror-womb'.[10] His choice of the word womb is loaded, and it highlights the silver mirror's implicit connection to Warhol's Factory (of course Klüver worked with Warhol, and EAT used to meet with Pepsi reps at the Electric Circus). But Youngblood's terminology points to the ways in which the pavilion extends the Silver Factory into an even more counterintuitive space for production: the shift from factory to artificial womb resulted in a progressively more extreme erasure of building. The corners, plumbing and structural beams of the Factory were silverised and hence pressed into service in support of a visual logic that disregarded their architectural functions, but they were nevertheless visible. In contrast, not only was the pavilion memberless, its curvature created the illusion of a complete world of fluid and unstructured affect where the constantly agitated reflections that seemed to be the constituent elements of the space lent the whole evanescence. But Youngblood's use of the metaphor of the womb, even if unintentionally, refers to the fact that architecture has always been the mother of the arts, the place where new forms of experience are shaped and where mediums and disciplines come together to generate unexpected and at least initially unrecognisable species of creation.

Ironically, then, the seemingly universal tendency of contemporary observers to overlook the pavilion's mundane qualities as a building distracted everyone from developing a theory of architecture adequate to the project. This would have entailed a theory of architecture concerned with the pavilion's qualities rather than its buildinghood – which in turn would have reconfigured the definition of architectural disciplinarity. Ultimately, the pavilion was more than simply not a building. In detaching from the traditional definitions of building, it underwent the period's investigation of intermedia, performance and interdisciplinary genres to push through to a new form of architecture: the supercharged environment where optical and auditory noise produce spectacular experience but no legible content. Horizons and contours are suppressed while surfaces are textured, patterned and reflective, producing an atmospheric perspective or ambience that makes the reading of bounded volume impossible. Within what can thus no longer be considered space in a philosophical sense, a dense accumulation of animated images replaces the traditionally attentive and single viewer with crowdedness and motion. Together, these qualities engender all the effects of architecture without either a building as object or the essentialist positions to which such objects are traditionally attached.

The pavilion's reception has placed it outside the bounds of architecture, a rejection that indicates a stubborn and persistent rigidity in architecture as a critical and historical category. The project itself, however, belongs to a moment when the discipline of architecture was set on reinventing itself. Just as the Mylar dome was being filled with the fiery air of Santa Ana, fire was ravaging Rudolph's Art and Architecture building on the Yale campus, an event often framed as one of the first salvos of the student uprisings of 1968, as an attack on the excessive brutality of modern hardware, and as an effort to make architecture appear to exemplify this hardware and therefore deserve to be sent off and up in a cloud of smoke. But architecture wanted to go off and become a cloud, as can be plainly seen in the many mobile, inflatable and mind-bending scenarios

EAT Wind Tunnel Test,
Kyoto University, 1969

that were still possible in 1970, produced just adjacent to rather than within the discipline, with many of them possessing the same amorphous, elusive, almost placeless qualities Youngblood had recognised in the Santa Ana dome. Traditionally a means to locate architecture, place instead became independent from location, produced by a confluence of often heterogeneous and ephemeral forces. Releasing its grip on the building as object, it allowed architecture to operate more and more like a cloud, in the sense that Hubert Damisch describes: a 'phenomenon that eludes … any essentialist position'.[11]

Just as Andy Warhol dislocated painting when he, with the help of Klüver, said goodbye to painting by releasing Mylar 'clouds' from the Castelli Gallery, EAT registered this dislocation when it hid the pavilion in a cloud. On the other hand, simply hiding a building doesn't make architecture disappear. (Never mind that the fog sculpture was actually intended to be a sign for the building, so large as to be visible across the huge expanse of the Expo. And never mind, as well, that the fog sculpture worked for only a few days anyway, leaving the shell visible during most of the expo.) EAT called themselves anti-expo and linked this opposition to their desire for a pavilion they could evaporate, as though anti-expo and anti-architecture were synonyms.[12] But what was really cloudy was their critique, presumably of corporate authority, which was so vague that it needed to take cover in an attack on building. EAT needed, as did many artists of the period, a straw man – or rather straw building – to huff and puff at in order to camouflage their oversimplification of the relationship between architecture and the institutions it houses. In the same way, the real target at the New Haven protests – academic authority and in particular its political attachments at Yale – was lost in the smoke that merely momentarily conflated architecture with the Art and Architecture building and the concrete of that building with power itself. Architecture became the object to be destroyed in the culture of '68. If the pavilion's contribution to architecture has not been recognised, it has also evaded these attacks on architecture for the same reasons. The fog may have merely covered its shell, but the atmosphere it contained was so elusive that it still hasn't even been acknowledged as architecture.

Building has traditionally been assigned the job of keeping out the rain, but architecture loves a cloud. From Brunelleschi's famous perspective apparatus, which captured the movement of a cloud in a burnished mirror, to Wölfflin's impassioned interest in the effects of chiaroscuro, to the atmospheric spectacle characterising the work of contemporary architects such as Herzog & de Meuron and Sanaa, the traces of weather have permitted architecture to animate otherwise inert building materials. These programmable effects do not oppose or merely supplement architecture; they are not software to its hardware but rather are its inhabitants or spectatorial stand-ins, witnesses to the passing cloud on Brunelleschi's mirror and to that moment in which perspective seemed, like a hologram, true to life. This was modern architecture's original place, neither a site nor a region, but a landscape of events wherein the visibility of individual constituent objects became clouded by their performance within a manifold ecology. The still unrecognised atmospheric architecture at Osaka was not the cloud stuck to the structure but the idea of organising the pavilion's entire mise-en-scène as a system of nebulous animations.

Architecture became cloud-like when it abandoned the autonomy of building to enter an ecological paradigm, which entailed giving up the clarity of modernism's straight lines and defined volumes but brought with it a new form of liveness. Pearce, in fact, did not consider the pavilion a place to be inhabited or something to look at but something itself already and always alive.[13] Klüver, too, argued that the Osaka Expo's most contemporary quality

EAT Pepsi Dome contact sheet, 1969

was not its showing of technology but its focus on the interaction between event and environment.[14] EAT staged this conversion from optics to ecology by first invoking building as the most concrete and visible form of objecthood and then making it vanish into the atmosphere. But in order to perform this transubstantiation, EAT had to frame architecture as an image of hardware. This projection, in turn, allowed them to imagine that their software could split off, somehow remaining free from the complicities that burden building. The culture of '68 underwrote its move into environments through an assault on architecture as a stand in for authority itself – as though museums and galleries were merely buildings that could be made to disappear. Artists misidentified architecture as something necessarily regional, that is fixed in place and fixes things in place, unable to see that their target had long since drifted off. In retrospect, only Allan Kaprow seems to have noticed, perhaps having trained himself to 'see' invisible architecture through his work on Fluids, his 1967 architectural happening in which he enlisted the help of passersby to build 15 houses of ice around Los Angeles – houses that melted away in a matter of hours. His proposal for a programme to take place in the pavilion – one of many EAT solicited as part of their plan to have a changing series of events over the course of the expo rather than a fixed installation – was called 'Heavenly Pastime in the Year 2000'. It transformed the pavilion's interior into a video game where visitors with light guns shot at virtual balls moving through the space (created by light interacting with the holographic effects of the mirror dome) until their allotted time was up and a voice summarised their performance: 'Ladies and Gentlemen. You are Group number 239. You have scored 46 direct hits, 122 near misses.' [15] His attack at least understood the nature of its target, which included not just the gun but the shooter and everything in between, not just the building but the architecture – an ecology as elusive as a cloud and as quixotic as the Santa Ana winds.

FLASH IN THE PAN

NOTES

1. Raymond Chandler's short story, *Red Wind*, was originally published in the January 1938 issue of *Dime Detective*.

2. Despite a growing literature on both EAT and the Osaka Expo, the most essential source on the Pepsi Pavilion in particular remains Billy Klüver, Julie Martin and Barbara Rose (eds), *Pavilion by Experiments in Art and Technology* (New York: EP Dutton & Co, 1972). Even this work, however, contains relatively little discussion of the tests done in Santa Ana. A great deal of primary documentation, however, on which much of this discussion is based, is contained in the EAT archive held at the Getty Research Institute. A significant number of photographs that document the trial, and its failure, are included. In addition, Eric Saarinen made a documentary film that contains extensive footage of the test. See his *The Great Big Mirror Dome Project*, 1969, film, 16 mm.

3. For the precise chronology of EAT's involvement, see Nilo Lindgren, 'Into the Collaboration', in *Pavilion*, 4ff.

4. Several different logos were designed. The focus of the variations is on both increasing the abstraction of the logo itself as well as on what materials should be used in order to make the logo adhere to Mylar. Although the final scheme no longer uses the blue and red of the classic Pepsi logo, an image of the pavilion becomes instead the logo's primary icon. For preliminary drawings, material samples and correspondence pertaining to the logo, see Getty Archive, Box 50 and Box 44, 6–12. The sheer quantity of material concerning something that was never used is telling in and of itself.

5. Issues of copyright are discussed at length in much of the correspondence about contracts and agreements between EAT and PepsiCo. See Getty Archive, Box 43, particularly files 1–8.

6. See notes in the Getty Archive, Box 44, file 27 as well as press release material about the test.

7. Robert Whitman was particularly concerned with this aspect of the interior. See, for example, the discussion in *Pavilion*, 14. On Whitman and the Pavilion, see Branden Joseph, 'Plastic Empathy: The Ghost of Robert Whitman', *Grey Room* 25 (Fall 2006), 64–91.

8. This discussion is based on a telephone interview I conducted with Pearce on 17 October 2006. He also contributed a first-person account of his involvement in *Pavilion* and the archive has extensive holdings of drawings he produced and supervised.

9. See *Pavilion*, 19.

10. Gene Youngblood, *Expanded Cinema*, 416.

11. See Hubert Damisch, 'Blotting Out Architecture? A Fable in Seven Parts', *Log* I (Fall 2003), 9–25.

12. Pearce seemed particularly acute to the difference between an architect and an artist's relationship to the institutions involved in the expo. He describes this anti-expo aspect of what he considered to be the intentions of the artists in his discussion in *Pavilion*, especially 256.

13. See *Pavilion*, 259 and 265.

14. See an interview with Klüver published in the *Asahi* newspaper, 27 June 1999 and held in the Getty Archive, Box 43, file 35.

15. Kaprow's proposal can be found along with approximately 50 others in the Getty Archive, Box 45, files 1–6.

SUPERCHARGED (2003)

In 1963 Bernard Rudofsky was working on *Architecture without Architects*, a project that included both a book and an exhibition that would open at the Museum of Modern Art in New York in the following year.[1] Just as early writers on the avant-garde understood Bohemia to be both a geographical and conceptual space of cultural exile, Rudofsky situated his study of a counter or primitivist avant-garde in what he called non-pedigreed architecture – outside traditional frames of reference. He focused mainly on historical vernaculars from across the globe not only because they tended to be located beyond the typically European centres of architectural discourse but also because they raised issues of material systems, ecology and collective life that did not fall within established historical and theoretical paradigms.[2] In the decades following Rudofsky's publication, which became a bestseller, Peter Eisenman was known to push against this celebration of architecture without pedigree by referring to some of his colleagues as *architects without architecture*, a category that converted what he considered to be the implicit nostalgia of Rudofsky's position with explicit satire. Nevertheless, Eisenman's quip was predicated on a similar distinction between architecture as discipline and building as practice.[3]

While Rudofsky and Eisenman sat on either side of an apparently infinite divide, and while neither had much sympathy for the profession, both understood the terms of their opposition in the same way: disciplinarity was largely a historical and intellectual project while building was a material and social practice. Each architect thought one term should subsume the other but – even if only through this struggle for domination – each operated according to the premise that building and disciplinarity were inextricably and dialectically linked. This essay instead considers architecture without building – or *as if architecture* – under the premise that insisting on a link between building and architecture, whether building is conceived as practice or as conceptual model, has long been used to suppress the very developments that, if recognised, would be among the most significant disciplinary reconfigurations of the last half century.

In 1963 an as yet unknown student named John Pearce entered Yale's School of Architecture. Though he would achieve a level of notoriety within the decade as the official architect of the Pepsi Pavilion at the 1970 Osaka Expo, his first job upon graduating was less highly visible:

Paul Rudolph
Apartment, NYC, 1967

he went to work for the outgoing Dean, Paul Rudolph, assuming responsibility for constructing the built-ins of Rudolph's New York apartment. Built-ins offer architecture a system of double camouflage. They both conceal their content and are themselves concealed. By mid-century, built-ins had become an established technique for making things disappear and functioned as a crucial if under-theorised device in the increasingly dominant logic of the architectural surface. Just as Andy Warhol would inflate the reach of art when he used Mylar pillows – released from the Castelli Gallery – to say goodbye to painting, built-ins deflated the space of building to help usher in and model a new set of architectural potentialities.

During the rise of consumer culture, the proliferation of objects that demanded if not architectural attention then in which the surface functioned as a disguise rather than a transparent plane, as it had in the first decades of the century. 'Things' increasingly came to be placed inside storage units that masqueraded as undecorated wall planes. The need to conceal things in order to ensure that interiors appeared to be modern ultimately undid the *sachlichkeit* logic of the architecture these interiors were intended to protect. Postwar built-ins literally turned a core tenet of prewar modernism – Adolf Loos's mandate that facades be blank so that interiors could be expressive – inside out and upside down. If Loos felt that a building's exterior should be like a man's suit and an interior like a lady's boudoir, built-ins hug a building's intimate inside parts like nude underwear: neither proper nor expressive, but confounding and alluring. In contrast to the componentry that structured Rietveld's Schroeder house, which functioned as small-scale building elements, colour-coded so that they not only reveal themselves but make their adherence to architectural logic as clear as possible, postwar built-ins lack visible hardware, distinguishing materials or colour, and legible contours. Like the shag carpet and seamless moulded plastic furniture that also became *de rigueur* during the 1960s and 70s, built-ins make building joints and all other architectural specificities perform a disappearing act, so the material of their surface is visible but reveals nothing.

A lot was hidden in Rudolph's apartment – most notably his lover, who slid in and out of a built-in closet tucked inside the apartment as a whole. Elaborately designed and constructed of both visually and structurally dense materials, the closet was otherwise completely invisible to anyone apart from Rudolph himself.[4] Perhaps under the pressure of these secrets, and perhaps even unbeknownst to Rudolph, the built-ins proliferated until they became the thing itself. The penthouse, which Rudolph drew as if it were a small, free standing multi-floor structure, operates less as a building and more as a pile of built-ins ungoverned by either the structural or compositional systematicity at work in the Schroeder house. If built-ins began as a way to make interior furnishings submit to architectural regulations by emphasising the abstraction of the wall and the purity of the space walls constructed, they did this job so well that they ultimately developed their own system with a logic that belongs neither to architecture nor to furniture. Instead, built-ins construct an architectural interior that is isomorphic with, but independent from, the building envelope, a quasi-autonomy that enables their surfaces to sidestep the obligation to reveal architecture in favour of becoming surfaces that are themselves the focus of attention and desire. Rather than architecture or decoration, built-ins construct a unified, uninterrupted plane of décor functioning *as if* it were architecture.

Much of Rudolph's work of the 1960s, in fact, is best understood as an accumulation of décor that rubs up against architecture's limits, swallows up its walls and makes building as such – its tectonics, volumes and logic – disappear. Indeed, a new kind of architecture emerged from this décor, which began with built-ins but quickly

Paul Rudolph,
Elman Apartment, NYC, 1971

moved into other forms of continuous, opaque, voluminous and enveloping surface: endless and thick piles of conversation pits and shag carpets, patterned and faceted shiny plastic, twinkling and twirling Mylar disks, even mirrors on strings, which multiplied and refracted everything in sight, exploding the interior in a dazzling display of exaggerated bewilderment. The interior was real, yet produced hallucinatory effects; the space was entirely usable, but equally nebulous. This was an architecture delaminated from the medium of building, not obligated to the logic of the visible and the verifiable (the only logic in which secrets can thrive); an architecture that instead sought to constitute itself through impressions, mirages and temptations and so offered not the abstractions of optical scenes but rather the sensation of dense haptic experience. The hyperactivated surfaces producing this rich if indefinable range of effects are *supercharged*, produced not by abstract planes but by systems of overlay laden with the weightless burden of the ineffable. By demanding visual attention without offering legibility, they supercharge the viewer, placing him or her in a state in which architecture performs as a palpably manifest substance instead of a detached and abstract system, while building moves in the opposite direction and fades into liminality.

In 1963 Andy Warhol began looking for a new workspace. In January 1964 he moved into a derelict building

on East 47th Street where Billy Linich, better known as Billy Name, soon covered the space in tinfoil and aluminium industrial paint, a combination he had first used in his downtown apartment.[5] It is said that the periodic repainting of the Mid-Hudson Bridge near his family home in Poughkeepsie inspired Billy's décor. But of course there were many examples of silverised architecture, from Richard Neutra, who had used

Billy Name, Andy Warhol at The Factory, c1964

paint on wood framing in most of his well-known mid-century houses in Los Angeles to Isamu Noguchi, whose own downtown studio was painted with aluminium paint at the suggestion of Buckminster Fuller.[6] But while an architect responding to such precedents would no doubt have understood that the aluminium in the paint had been intended to grant the painted surface the status of metal construction, Warhol and his peers read the aluminium paint and the tinfoil indiscriminately as silver.[7]

In other words, Warhol did not think of silver as a material, as an architect would understand the concept: none of the things he associated with the colour of the Factory – astronaut suits, the silver screen and mirrors – were actually made of silver in 1963. Instead, silver was an effect that, particularly when exaggerated by stage lights, animated the Factory's interior and made the ambience of the space itself a machine for producing endless, shifting images. As if to emphasise the nature of this apparitional environment, a disco ball – the quintessential proliferator and environmental diffuser of quasi-serial images – occupied a prominent position on the Factory floor.

The Factory was famously an environment for producing images – not just painting and silkscreens, but countless photographs and numerous films – and these pictures were predicated on the kind of extreme visibility that might be expected from such delirious effects. Someone was usually dressing or undressing, if not dressing up, and someone else was likely to be having sex for the camera. The door was generally left open. Nothing was hidden. Everything and everyone was always all too visible. Except, tellingly, one key element of this space remains historically obscured. The Factory is iconic in the history of art, but not in that of architecture. This oversight is no doubt because it lacks the characteristics of building: it does not rely on the instruments of architectural representation, it is too decorative, it cannot claim an architect as its author, it is insufficiently deliberate, and it produces its impact merely through the proliferation of images and ambient effects. The one thing hidden in and by the Factory was its architecture, as if the actual building was out-shadowed by Warhol's virtual one. Nevertheless, the Silver Factory had an architecture: not only did it actually belong to the historical building type of the factory, but it was a space designed to accommodate specific types of events and to encourage particular forms of social practice. What distinguishes the Silver Factory is that it produced the effect of architecture without the officiations of an architect and, more importantly, without the medium of building. It was made by covering up the building with visual performance: a supercharged surface *as if* architecture.

In 1963 Italian architect and designer Carlo Mollino discovered Polaroids.[8] He had always been interested in photography, and particularly their manipulation of the photographic image. He printed and retouched his own pictures prior to their exhibition, pictures that often depicted mirrors and reflective surfaces and so explored the spectacle of vision. Already in 1936 he had taken a photograph of a woman in a body-hugging, shiny silk negligee emerging from a closet filled to the brim with 'things'. Mollino went on to publish *Message from the Dark*

Room, one of the earliest histories of photography to focus on the photographer's capacity to falsify images.[9] But his encounter with the Polaroid released a fetish, quite impressive given that he was already famously overcome by fetishes ranging from racecars to aerial skiing. Upon his death in 1973, over 2,000 pornographic Polaroids of local prostitutes in various states of dress and undress were discovered hidden in a drawer in his studio.[10] The images were unsigned and unframed – Mollino died unexpectedly – and there is no evidence to suggest he intended them to be seen. While the women came from the streets, Mollino photographed them in a private world he designed around them. Before elaborately posing them in his own house, he costumed the girls, buying outfits in several sizes, some of which were even mail-ordered from Paris. Many of

Carlo Mollino,
untitled, c1968–73

the clothes, however, were more locally sourced. One of the most striking dresses was by Paco Rabanne, an architect who had left architecture for the more commercial, immediate and disposable world of fashion (where, appropriately, Polaroids were also enjoying great popularity as an expedient means for testing exposures and establishing visual continuity for the final images captured on regular film and photographic paper). The dress was most likely purchased in nearby Milan, possibly in a shop called Altre Cose designed by Ugo La Pietra, another ex-architect, and a future member of the radical but short-lived Italian design collective Global Tools.[11] Although it was considered the very epicentre of high fashion when it opened – composed of a sophisticated combination of new materials, technologies and programmes that together produced an environment of extreme effects almost unrivalled in contemporary European design – this boutique remains invisible to our understanding of the formation of contemporary architecture, much like the women in Mollino's Polaroids who were visible for a moment in the camera's flash but quickly receded into a secret drawer. Similar to Warhol's factory and Rudolph's apartment, it has been excluded from architectural history, not because it is an example of an architecture, without an architect or is a work of an architect without architecture but because it produces architectural effects without the crutch of building.

As worlds apart as the clean-cut Yale grad, the famously stylish artist and the mad race car driver from Turin may initially seem, and as outside the proper confines of architecture Mylar disks, acrylic tubes and sparkling tin foil may be, all offer an expanded understanding of architecture. The architecture found here – in the animated, reflective surface; in the surface without depth, which hides things with excess dazzle; in the surface that produces vivid but unclassifiable and hence hard-to-grasp images; and in unbounded environments held together by qualities rather than by legible limits – is architecture supercharged. It offers the means to rewrite the discipline's rules of attraction, but not simply by letting queerness, or fetishism or voyeurism out of the closet – nothing so legitimising as that. Indeed, most of this decorative, ephemeral, commercial and frivolous architecture is still quite illegitimate. And so to consider it today is not so much to argue that it had historical importance that has been neglected as to rekindle a furtive desire in the present. It is contemporary architecture, not architectural history, which ultimately produces the importance of this past. And architecture today needs this almost-architecture of 1963 to transcend those currents within the architectural profession (and increasingly in criticism as well) that still insist on establishing an equivalence between architecture and building, precisely because they so deeply fear being intoxicated by the immersive spectacle of intense architecture provocation.

The limits imposed by these doxa still form the core of prevalent critical discourse because their roots run deep into the history of modern aesthetics, one of the foundational acts of which was to separate beauty as such from beauty's capacity to arouse. Since Winckelmann's frankly erotic reading of young white boys was sublimated into ideal standards of abstract form, since Kant informed us that aesthetic appreciation of grapes entailed *not* feeling hunger even when contemplating their most luscious depiction, since Greenberg disparaged kitsch as overly abetting desire, any inadequate suppression of appetite, any soupcon of desire whetted, has been understood as evidence of weakness in the critic. But only in architecture has the complex intimacy between desire and beauty been so actively opposed that transgression demanded outright criminalisation: critics in and of the field are the strictest hall monitors, always on the look out for infractions. Loos's criminalisation of ornament – fuelled by his fear of the sexuality it might unleash – and Tafuri's condemnation of operative criticism as the handmaiden of capitalism are but two examples within an architectural discourse that continues to enforce a quasi-juridical system of norms against temptation, persuasion and pleasure.[12] And so the architect keeps a prophylactic nearby, often in the form of a sturdy building, so that things don't go all the way with surfaces and other apparent superficialities, just as any good critic of architecture must never show signs of having been seduced even by the idea of seduction. But if – according to Tafuri – allowing yourself to succumb to the wiles of seduction makes you operative, it follows that avoiding seduction makes you inoperative. Here are the dictionary definitions of inoperative: not functioning properly, not effective or no longer valid, out of action, out of order, out of use, broken, broken down.

Precisely why architectural criticism loves a taboo more than it loves an invitation and differs from criticism of other art practices largely because of this self-imposed punitive posture would be interesting to analyse, but whatever its etiology, the result has been to restrict rather than expand the field of architectural potentiality. La Pietra's Altre Cose is one victim of these taboos, of the field's unwillingness to see supercharged surfaces as architecture. Soon after it opened, the store was published

in leading Italian design magazines, like *Domus*, which
circulated widely in the 1960s and may even be considered
the publication of record for advanced European design,
and La Pietra achieved a degree of prominence. Critics
and visitors alike seemed to find the most fascinating
aspect of his design work in general to be what he called
his Disequilibriating System, which entailed a focus
on micro-environments in which light and sound were
manipulated to interrupt habitual sensory experience.[13]
Most of all, he was interested in patterns and in the ways
in which small deflections can entice a pattern, along with
the viewer or listener, into the random fluidity of three-
dimensional atmospheric perspective. Given contemporary
architects' interest in both these kinds of pattern problems
and the era of the late 1960s, it is surprising that Altre Cose
has not entered the record as one of the few built experiments in this mode of design. Ultimately, only the boutique's
frivolous lack of allegiance to the properties of building
explains why it lurks around like an embarrassing
proclivity, forever outside the margins of mainstream
architectural discourse.

Ironically, Altre Cose itself wasn't shy – its
look-up-your-skirt, peek-a-boo point of view marked an
approach to the theatre and sociality of shopping more
brazen than any current approach to the architecture
of fashion. There were two entrances to Altre Cose and
both were 'disequilibriating'. Street-level entry took place
through doors that opened electronically along opposing
diagonal vectors, skewing the initial understanding of
the organisation of the interior. The second and far more
impressively 'off-kilter' mode of entry – in an early example
of what the Italians call contaminated programming – took
place in an acrylic elevator that carried two people up
along an inclined track from the Bang Bang nightclub (the
first of its kind in Milan) located one level below the street.
The main space of the boutique was densely filled with
acrylic columns suspended from the ceiling that contained
a dazzling array of clothing: like the fashions designed
by Rabanne, these were mostly made of the same plastic

Ugo La Pietra, Altre Cose,
Milan, 1969

materials that laminated the store. Linking the body to its environment, a theme often discussed during the 1960s in architecture as well as in fashion, La Pietra fitted the interior of the store with sliding panels hand-drilled in optical patterns made out of pre-production plastic sheets used in making buttons.

Shoppers selected desired items from a computer console, which activated the column containing that particular article by first illuminating and then lowering the chosen cylinder to the floor. In descent, the reflective columns containing articles of clothing began to occupy the same space as – and to move alongside – shoppers wearing the clothing. The net result was a mingling of architecture and bodies, a crowd of girls in dresses and dresses without girls that was phantasmagorically doubled by a rear mirror-wall.

The invisibly architectural status of La Pietra's design can be calibrated by considering his scheme's obvious reference to Giuseppe Terragni's well-known Danteum. Both are divided into three levels, organised around a circuit that ascends from darkness to light, and conclude in a hypostyle hall of transparent columns. But La Pietra's paraphrase utterly expels the poetic and architectural gravitas of Terragni's project, treating this forcefully emptied out container as something to fill with a gaseous cloud made of an infinite number of agitated particles of light and sound. Where Terragni offered sacred geometry, hermeneutic interpretation and narrative purpose, La Pietra presents random events and movements, spectacle and distortion. Indeed, critic Gillo Dorfles wrote at the time that La Pietra had suppressed traditional forms of content by deliberately manufacturing noise.[14] Germano Celant, in turn, maintained that this noise increased the aesthetic impact of La Pietra's work by distracting the viewer from any single sense and encouraging him or her to feel multiple components of the sensory apparatus fire simultaneously. And according to *Domus*, La Pietra and his architecturally trained colleagues like Paco Rabanne and Quasar Khanh were showing fashion design what to learn from the noise, distractions and behavioural multiplicities that characterise architectural spaces and urban environments.[15] Rather than architects trying to keep up with the pace of fashion – and being habitually condemned for these efforts – in the 1960s the reverse argument was made: that by using surfaces to engage passive users and transform them into active and collective participants, architects – or architectural thinking – were making culture that was responsive and environmental rather than static and autonomous. This radical shift in the conceptualisation of the duration of cultural objects came from within architecture and from within architecture's internally driven transformation of its spatial medium. Rather than produce a new style, architecture was engaging with the conditions by which style changed, and thereby with the conditions by which fashion could produce the notion – and the speed – of the fashionable. Fashionability is an architectural concept.

For Celant, the intersection between fashion and architecture in the work of La Pietra and others created a new category of aesthetic experience. With all due attention to its oxymoronic impossibility, he called it fruitful, or useful, pleasure: *piacevolezza fruitiva*. Utility was derived from the environmental capacity of clothing and architecture: they could be worn and used. The pleasure came from visually animated design. But for Celant, immersion in such a multiplex environment was exponentially pleasurable. The noisy ambience produced consumers who participated in the act of consumption not through the traditional solitary contemplation of a distant aesthetic object but rather in terms of epicentric and communal excitement. For Celant, in other words, a place like Altre Cose was itself aesthetically 'supercharged'. This was perhaps nowhere more true than in the dressing room – called an undressing room in Italian – where everyone undressed and dressed back up together, in full view of and often in close proximity to each other, a room covered in angled sparkly surfaces. Significantly, La Pietra did not include drawings of this room when he published Altre Cose. The simplest explanation for this omission is that changing rooms are programmatically beneath the need for architectural representation, even for architects working outside such architectural conventions. But it may also have been that its highly active visual qualities were beyond the capacity of architectural drawings during that period – indeed were resistant to architectural representation – and were better captured in the *punctum* of a photograph. Whatever the reason for its obscurity, this secret closet of immersive, kaleidoscopic intensity turns out to be the place where the distinction collapses between Mollino Polaroids of prostitutes hidden away in a drawer, and a new generation of architectural users seeking *piacevolezza*.

Architecture has traditionally not had a good place to put such appetites. Indeed the history of the postwar era has been written with strict attention to steadfast refusniks of commerce and commodity. But the era also has an unwritten history, that of a new generation of users who had LSD and birth control, and who wanted architecture to be an element of their intoxication. As is their obligation, contemporary works demand a new canon (or anti-canon) to use as precedent or alibi and in fact a wide range of current architectural obsessions – animated surfaces, supercharged effects, immersive environments – come together in a virtually unknown series of almost-architectures from this period of lustful appetites. Indeed, there was nothing historic about 1963. On the contrary: contemporary work is conjuring up these events, making it both possible and necessary to see Warhol's silver, Rudolph's Mylar, Mollino's French lace and La Pietra's wild acrylics. These old works are today's urgings for architecture to behave in ways that exceed or escape expectation – enticements to accept the idea that architecture can participate in the culture of appetites, rather than remain in its traditional role as appetite suppressant, and still be architecture. But while some architects are becoming flirtatious, they hesitate to consummate the act. Self-imposed censorship reintroduces the familiar constraints of programme and content, of utility without *piacevolezza*. Today, as repression and prohibition are becoming as rampant in culture at large as they have long been in architecture, it is more important than ever to insist that even something as apparently stolid as a familiar building can become new and better when seduced into changing its colours.

NOTES

1. The catalogue was published as *Architecture Without Architects: A Short Introduction to Non-Pedigreed Architecture* (New York, NY: MoMA, 1965). On Rudofsky, see *Lessons from Rudofsky: Life as a Voyage*, catalogue of a 2007 exhibition held at the Architekturzentrum Wien and published in association with the Getty Research Institute, as well as Felicity Scott, 'Underneath Aesthetics and Utility: The Untransposable Fetish of Bernard Rudoskfy', *Assemblage* 38 (April 1999), 58–89.

2. Rudosfky borrowed the term non-pedigree as well as many of the images in *Architecture Without Architects* from the Swiss photographer Martin Hürlimann. Interestingly enough, Robert Venturi also used many of Hürlimann's images in *Complexity and Contradiction*, which establishes Hürlimann as the foundational link between Rudofsky's non-pedigree and Venturi's ordinary architecture and suggests the important role of the photo-survey in establishing a frame, as it were, within which architecture and building could coincide. On Bohemia as the site of the birthplace of the avant-garde, see Clement Greenberg, 'Avant-Garde and Kitsch', in *Partisan Review* 6:5 (Fall 1939).

3. To my knowledge Eisenman has never written about this subject directly, although I (along with others) have heard him make this remark on several occasions.

4. On this aspect of the penthouse, see Tim Rohan, 'Public and Private Spectacles: Paul Rudolph's Manhattan Penthouse, 1977–1999', *Casabella* December 1999, 138–49.

5. On Billy Name's role in the Factory, see Steven Watson, *Factory Made: Warhol and the Sixties* (New York, NY: Pantheon Books, 2003).

6. Noguchi returned the 'silverising' favour and made a bust of Fuller out of chrome nickel steel used by Henry Ford in the Model A. On their relationship, see Shoji Sadao, *Buckminster Fuller and Isamu Noguchi: Best of Friends* (New York, NY: Isamu Noguchi Foundation, 2011).

7. In an email sent to me on 13 March 2007, Billy Name wrote, 'I considered the silverising of the factory overall to be an "installation" in the art genre sense. Having been trained as a lighting designer and stage manager for theater and dance I was used to designing an entire area (stage set).'

8. The reception and historiography of Mollino is full of gaps and contradictions, but the basic literature includes *Carlo Mollino, Architetto, Construire le modernita* (Milan: Electa, 2006) and Giovanni Brino, *Carlo Mollino: Architecture as Autobiography: Architecture, Furniture, Interior Design, 1928–1973* (New York, NY: Rizzoli, 1987).

9. See Carlo Mollino, *Il Messaggio Dalla Camera Oscura* (Turin: Chiantore, 1949).

10. The Polaroids were published in *Carlo Mollino: Polaroids* (Santa Fe, NM: Arena Press, 2002).

11. Altre Cose was the hub of high-end progressive fashion in Milan, precisely the kind of only a very small number of shops that would have carried such an advanced dress. This kind of clothing was often seen in magazines but not that widely available for purchase.

12. Of course the classic statement within architectural discourse of the eroticisation of denial is Adolf Loos's 'Ornament and Crime [1909]', *Ornament and Crime*, trans Michael Mitchell (Riverside, CA: Ariadne Press, 2002), 167–76.

13. La Pietra's investigations were in close dialogue with Claude Parent's better-known contemporary invention of what he called the Function of the Oblique. See his *The Function of the Oblique: The Architecture of Claude Parent and Paul Virilio 1963–1969* (London: AA Publications, 2004).

14. See Ugo La Pietra, Gillo Dorfles and Daniela Palazzoli, *Il systema disequilibrante* (Genoa: Masnata, 1971) and La sinestesia delle arti, (Milan: Mazzotta, 2001).

15. See 'Un architetto per vestire la moda: La boutique "Altre Cose" a Milano', *Domus* 460 (March 1968), 32–37.

THE TURN-ON (2001)

In 1976 Reyner Banham retroactively described the
South Bank Exhibition, which had been the centrepiece
of the massive 1951 Festival of Britain, as 'a turn-on'.[1]
This is scarcely what the Labour party had in mind when
they organised it; they intended to tell a grand story of
British achievement, providing the nation with a much-
needed boost to its morale in the grim early years of
postwar recovery. The festival was enormously well
attended during its five-month span, and initially seemed
to accomplish the goal of modernising British culture and
updating it for the postwar era. Its so-called contemporary
style and aesthetic, everything from the typography used
in its signage and promotional materials to its treatment
of landscape, was widely and immediately disseminated
through media coverage and much of its visual vocabulary
was replicated and mass produced in textiles, furnishings
and every conceivable appurtenance. The architectural
ambitions of the South Bank Exhibition in particular were
impressively high. Numerous noted architects participated,
including Maxwell Fry and Wells Coates, not only
introducing a then still unfamiliar international style
modernism to Britain but collectively making a euphoric
claim to offer the first built glimpse into what a fully
modern European city might look like.[2]

But this popular success turned out to be a
momentary interlude on the festival's path towards almost
instantaneous critical failure, as its utopian rhetoric was
quickly recast as palaver intended to seduce the public
into embracing not so much the historical ambitions
of modernism as the emerging logic of consumer culture.
Only one month after its closing, the festival came to be

described as flimsy and effeminate or, in the words of artist Richard Hamilton, 'merely corridor after corridor of frilly whimsy'.[3] Once the crowds had left, it became possible to see that the foundations of a modernist city had not been laid, and no substantial impact on architecture been achieved or even anticipated. Instead of a robust transfor-mation in building, all that remained was the consumerist flotsam and jetsam that Hamilton and his peers in Britain's emerging pop movement were already critiquing. In the face of such acerbic rejection, it is no wonder that the event is now virtually invisible to architectural and design history, except as a periodic reminder of modernism's disfigurement by the consumer-driven culture of postwar reconstruction.

Indeed, when Banham attempted to redeem the festival in the 70s, he was careful to recover its ambiance rather than its architecture, which he dismissed as 'died-a-borning'. For Banham, the festival had a productive impact, not because it had permitted modern architecture to achieve maturity, but because it coincided with the burgeoning of a youth culture that would ultimately engage with the visual field in a new way, relatively unconcerned with traditional or even typically modernist formal systems. The general public that had gorged on the festival atmosphere would have included, so Banham speculated, young people like the future members of Archigram, with the potential but not yet the training to become innovative architects. That they were not yet architects was essential to Banham's understanding of the importance of the festival because they would have visited the South Bank as unwitting participants with a pre-architectural consciousness rather than as professional observers. They were thus blind to the festival's stylistic improprieties but fully amenable to being turned on by its heady atmosphere.

For Banham the festival was a failure on the level of buildings but a significant event nonetheless, because it had demonstrated that architecture could achieve its effects by working indirectly through an overall gestalt rather than directly through legible form. On the one hand this indirection enabled Banham to reinforce his often stated frustration with what he considered to be the myopia of the architectural discipline: describing a success that a traditionally trained architectural expert could not recognise was less an endorsement of the success as such than an ironic critique of the particular form of blindness produced by so-called expert training. On the other hand, and however much Banham wished to mythologise the generation that had in fact become prominent architects by the time of his commentary, the ability to perceive what the experts failed to see was not the result of the acumen of innocent eyes. Instead, the festival's capacity to function as a turn-on not only relied on an audience seeking to be electrified but was in fact more related to its actual staging of architecture than Banham allowed. The youth of 1951 received the festival through indirect and distracted attention, but the festival also presented itself in forms that were resistant to then-dominant conventions of modern opticality.

The South Bank Exhibition was a tangle of exfoliating buildings, each losing its physical and formal autonomy in a plethora of out-rigged structures and surface agitations.

The plan was congested and lacked a clear promenade, with each pavilion bumping up against the next. Landscaping and street furniture clogged open space, such that there was never any possibility of backing up far enough to get a proper view. Nor were the buildings staged for posterity.

View of the Festival of Britain, 1951

The South Bank was unphotogenic, even by the relatively low-resolution standards of the day. Period photographs, despite the wide range of equipment used, consistently betray a camera with bad vision, situated too close to show buildings, too low to show the complex, and too far away to show details. Neither the festival nor its representations had what just a few years later Kevin Lynch called imageability, and thus could not – and still cannot – be seen properly. The festival was a blur that was unable – or refused – to cohere into a legible structure.[4] And yet while this lack of optical finality condemned it to historical failure, forestalling its capacity to be visually fixed and hence its capacity to be fixed in memory and to enter the canon, it also generated the promiscuous visuality that led Banham to call it a turn-on. The festival permitted Banham to bemoan the blindness of the old experts while celebrating the blindness of the young because between 1951 and 1976 the terms of architectural evaluation had changed, shifting their focus from the formal clarity of brick and mortar buildings to architecture's capacity to engage subjects indirectly through atmosphere.

In 1973 interior designer Barbara D'Arcy left Bloomingdales, where she had been on the staff since 1952.[5] She began her tenure as a junior decorator in the fabric department but ultimately oversaw the redesign of the entire flagship store, selected Massimo Vignelli to design the store's graphic programme, including the now iconic shopping bag, directed the company's expansion into a suburban network of visually linked shops and, most importantly in this context, designed over a hundred model rooms for the furniture department. Much more than an arrangement of objects in quasi-realistic settings – the

Barbara D'Arcy, *The Bloomingdale's Book of Home Decorating*, 1973

typical way to market furniture – these were highly elaborated installations, cordoned zones of often fantastic design. *The New York Times* noted her departure specifically in relation to these rooms by wondering if crowds of her fans would still make their 'pilgrimages to the decorated model rooms she had made so famous... [and] filled with the mystique that kept Park Avenue dinner parties buzzing and fashionable people dropping by'.[6] Not only were the rooms discussed at parties, but they were themselves occasions for sociability, to use sociologist Georg Simmel's term for those moments when individuals are converted into a free and amicable collective interaction that he characterised as having aesthetic charm. D'Arcy's model rooms were settings for what was nicknamed Saturday's Generation, after the upscale crowd who came to Bloomingdale's on Saturdays not only to see what was new and for sale, but specifically to lounge in her environments. The rooms were not themselves for sale but were an important staging ground for the constitution of a new relationship between the momentary formations of social life and the temporality of architecture.

Although retail design is now recognised as a site of artistic invention of sorts, D'Arcy herself has remained largely anonymous. Like the historical invisibility of the Festival of Britain, her auratic failure can also be understood as an inevitable consequence of both her design and the conditions in which it was received. On the one hand the model rooms were temporary, commercial, composed of a heterogeneous assemblage of found, designed and fabricated objects, hugely varied in style and associated mostly with domestic decoration.

Any one of these characteristics is enough to render the model rooms crimes against modern design, but all of them together has undoubtedly been considered a capital offence, killing any capacity of D'Arcy to be constituted as an author. On the other hand there is also enough continuity between one model room and another for a coherent design strategy to be extrapolated from them as a whole. Regardless of what she was displaying, two techniques always guided her *mises-en-scène*. First, all surfaces are rendered continuously: there is never a blank spot, only uninterrupted, enveloping saturation of colour, material or lighting effects. Second, 'original' objects, in this case off-the-shelf products available for purchase in the store, ranging from modern furnishings from Herman Miller and Kartell to more traditional furniture designs, to one-of-a-kind rarities she brought back from her travels, were then mixed together with what she called 'interpretations', appurtenances and objects of various sorts, from wall hangings to chairs that she had made because she thought they were necessary to complete the environment.[7] One of D'Arcy's later model rooms, from 1972, combined all these strategies in a tour de force of monolithic design, when she chose to feature Frank Gehry's newly launched line of cardboard furniture, Easy Edges, in a fully cardboard environment made of tables and chairs in production, a one-off bed produced especially for the occasion, and a series of walls and platforms all made in the manner of the chairs.[8] In other words, the need to constitute a credibly coherent ambience overrode the need to use the retail floor to sell or authenticate goods.

The result of D'Arcy's combination of saturation with miscegenation is twofold. First, the distinction between figure and ground dissolves into a unified surface and the whole environment becomes a décor rather than a space with things in it. In fact her rooms reactivate a long neglected genealogy of décor, a term that originates in the eighteenth century. Before then, interior surfaces were tended to and distinguished by various crafts – woodworkers for floors, upholsterers for furniture and drapes, stucco-workers for ceilings. Each surface corresponded to a distinct material and form of production and each was individually considered to be a decorative art. Beginning with the rococo, these separate spheres of artisanal practice were not only elaborated but proliferated until they covered virtually the entire interior surface.[9] At this juncture, the decorative arts merged into an overall system and *les arts décoratifs* (plural) became *le décor* in the singular. Ironically, since architects later condemned this transformation of decoration into an architectural force, the development of décor relied on a single manager who oversaw the unification of these various crafts and that person was most often an architect. Twentieth-century notions of total environment, unbeknownst to their protagonists, would have been inconceivable without the decoration that was the very first medium to constitute the interior as a total ambient environment.

The second significant consequence of generating an environment by total décor is that the autonomy of objects as such is weakened. Even though the Anna Castelli storage units manufactured by Kartell or the Gehry Easy Edges were well on their way to becoming icons collected and displayed in museums by the time they were shown at Bloomingdales, D'Arcy's installations dissipate their singularity in a way that is anathema to either the museum effect or the aura needed by icons. Just as the Gehry chairs melded into a total a universe of cardboard, Castelli's units were stacked in so many piles, and the piles were in turn cast in so much coloured light that no one unit is visually separable from the whole. In these rooms, individual objects, individuated authors and, indeed, individuals joined what Simmel described as a higher social unity.[10] This dissolution of the object, in other words, had the most profound implication for the sociability engendered by these rooms, for when the individual thing dissolved into the décor so too did the individual subject; filled with Saturday's Generation, these rooms became participatory stagings, *mises-en-scène* of performers and props in which distinct identities faded into the sociable temporality of an afternoon occasion.

If Banham was turned on by atmosphere a few years after D'Arcy disappeared in Bloomie's décor, a few years earlier still, in 1967, *House Beautiful* had announced the arrival of what the magazine editors called 'turned-on' décor.[11] They described a growing tendency to adopt for

private use projective devices previously used primarily for stage and display windows, then most famously at clubs like the Electric Circus, which they cited in particular. The result was a new trend in apartments and home interiors, wherein floors, ceilings and walls – all available surfaces, in fact – were suddenly charged with an electrically powered 'high fantasy.' The interest of such projects lay in the totality of their décor, as well

C Ray Smith Apartment, New York City, 1967

as in the instantaneousness of projective animation, its capacity suddenly to be turned on, abruptly switching the cadence of architecture from space to event.[12]

Although *House Beautiful* was scarcely a radical magazine, the editors were precocious in having recognised a trend that was not only rapidly leaving behind its immediate source in theatre design, but that would quickly grow beyond the domestic interior as well. Over the course of a few short years, projection became internationally pervasive and particularly transformative for architectural practices interested in rethinking the experience of media at the scale of the city.[13] For example, in 1968, and more precisely from 11pm to 12pm on 25 September, the Italian collective Gruppo 9999 (the most junior group to be included in the exhibition Italy: The New Domestic Landscape held at the MoMA a few years later) projected a shifting montage of images – juxtaposing abstract effects

Gruppo 9999, Urban Decoration (Projectual Happening), Florence, 1968

of light and colour with LA freeways, astronauts and other techno-futuristic subjects – onto the Ponte Vecchio in Florence for an audience that stood on the banks of the Arno.[14] As the old bridge got turned on, a once heavy thoroughfare became a light node in a global, even extraterrestrial, transportation system. The projected images transported the Ponte Vecchio itself across space and time, and the event as a whole became an urban transporter using animated urban infrastructure to carry spectators to a new order in which architecture was identified by time rather than place. As unlikely as the collapse of past and present, close and far might have appeared on that evening in 1968, it reflected the actual reconfiguration of space and time being established by the global spread of new technologies. Indeed, the projected images used by the Florentine group recapitulate Banham's book of the same year, *The Architecture of the Well-Tempered Environment*, which argued that advances in mechanical systems were leading to a newly adaptable architecture that could expand to the scale of Las Vegas, which after all was an entire city made atmospherically coherent through the outdoor use of electric light, or retract to the scale of an individual living pod or suit that could appear at any time and in any place.[15]

If both Gruppo 9999 and Banham were, in different ways, turning architecture on by exploring the idea that buildings and cities were being transformed into an environmental apparatus – whether a superstructure for projection or an atmospheric envelope – then the Los Angeles-based collective Environmental Communications (EC) was pushing this same line of experimentation to its limit, envisioning an architecture fully turned on. A now largely forgotten team of architects, planners, photographers, historians, artists and marketers, EC was formed in 1969 by the architect David Greenberg in association with the photographer Roger Webster.[16] Deeply influenced by the theories of Marshall McLuhan, the group set out to explore the implications for contemporary spatial experience of the increasing media saturation. At first concerned primarily with using Los Angeles as a case study, they used photography and videography to document billboards, contemporary architecture, street art, pop art, mobile homes and *truchitecture* (EC's neologism for trucks so elaborated and lived in by their drivers that they became quasi-buildings). But what they ultimately produced was an almost infinite stream of images that together constituted an image of the turned-on city. Their goal, in other words, was not to make buildings or works of art but rather to disseminate a concept of environment as made up of every piece of data, matter and energy within the visual field.

Throughout the 1970s Environmental Communications produced slides, film and video of everything from pollution to the television environment, everywhere from Osaka to India, until they had captured thousands of images that constituted the pixels of the global information environment. Their projects relied on pre-digital crowd sourcing, in which they harnessed a massive and always fluctuating group of people to produce catalogues, brochures and, most importantly, the packaged sets of photographic slides that were distributed by mail. Unlike typical photographic archives, which generally sold the right to reproduce images in publication, the images held by Environmental Communications were often sold to schools of architecture, where they were folded into slide libraries and used in teaching. In fact, these slide sets of phenomena did more than create an enormous dispersed and mobile visual databank: they were originators of discourse going far beyond the standard architectural curriculum, the infrastructure for a new architecture of communication. The apparatus constructed by EC relied on a delirium-inducing record of volatile events, information flows and technological ruptures to generate architecture, to build architecture, using only projected images as its medium and a collective conversation as its programme.

While related to the widespread use of projection technologies in the 1960s, which has been broadly discussed in art and cultural histories, the specifically architectural implications of turned-on décor have gone largely unnoticed. First, architecture becomes a filmic apparatus, as images are projected directly onto walls without screens. In the extreme case of EC, architecture might disappear entirely, replaced by anything from a physical object such as a truck to a media campaign like a circulating catalogue. Second, its atmospheric elasticity puts pressure on the distinction that architecture has traditionally made between public and private space. For EC, such divisions melted into the enveloping ether of media; in the Florentine happening, the images implicated both urban and personal space; *House Beautiful* pointed out that projections were ideal 'for a party or for your own delight'; in a D'Arcy environment, the projection takes place in a domestic setting on commercial display; even for Banham the rigid spatial (and implicitly social) hierarchies of modernism could be melted away by projection. Rather than existing singularly as public or private, exhibition, apartment, bridge, showroom, and architectural classroom were organised around sociabilities determined by performativity: regardless of where or with whom the observer stood, the ontology of self ceased to be either singular or an a priori and became instead a function of the illumination of stage lights. Or as *Domus* argued in a similar context, as an 'electrically extended architecture', turned-on décor was best considered an environment of 'now and then', neither an open nor closed space but rather an environmental mode that flickers between on or off.[17]

If turned-on décor uses projection to produce architecture as atmosphere, it also links architecture to the plastic nature of sociability rather than to stabilising spatial or programmatic structures. This double subversion and radicalisation of architectural expectation helps explain why the history of turned-on décor remains little known. An equally important and related factor in the relative obscurity of these projects is their temporality: the suddenness with which they were turned off and on refused those forms of permanence that remain prerequisites for entering architecture's historical record. As a result, the turn-on is not only a spatial and architectural concept, but a temporal and historical one too. The issue is not, then, whether or not these projects had an impact during their brief lives; all of them had their 15 minutes of fame and most were widely publicised, in fact. Yet their notoriety often seemed as short-lived as the projects themselves, which often lasted only 30 minutes (at most five months) – a blink of an eye in architectural time. Since the pulsing atmospherics by which they were constituted were formally evanescent and hard to grasp, and since they were also literally temporary, the projects have no durable historical or material value. Fundamentally, then, these projects – occupied by performing participants and consumers rather than by observers or users – emerge from the logic of 15 minutes of fame, from an incompatibility with permanence as well as with memory, from heady atmospheres rather than stable and legible spaces. These projects are exemplary Flashes in the Pan.

The flash in the pan is an abject form of modern duration, conjuring the humiliating anxiety of becoming a has-been. Modernity may have had an apparent interest in the throwaway, the popular and up-to-datedness, but it also retained an underling investment in the absolute, the refined and the lasting. In the context of these values, the flash in the pan inevitably signals failure, especially to architecture, whose self-image is as the very arbiter of permanence. Yet the flash in the pan is also a peculiarly modern form of achievement for which architecture – forced by its very durability to seek out compensatory forms of contemporaneity – offers a surprisingly acute means of analysis. The term derives from an actual misfire (when the priming powder of a musket goes off in the pan but does not ignite the charge in the bore, so that the gun does not shoot). But rather than a non-event, the flash in the pan might be best understood as a spectacular failure that produces a sudden brilliance, blinding if short-lived.

The flash in the pan and turned-on architecture are logically resonant concepts: just as Gruppo 9999's happening was over almost before it began, its disorienting atmospheric complexity impossible to document and nearly as difficult to recall, the flash in the pan is not something forgettable, per se. Rather, it is an event that produces invisibility *as effect*, an event that actively makes itself hard to remember. Reciprocally constituted across a duration paradoxically without time and through a spectacle paradoxically without seeing, the flash in the pan is thus resistant both to memory and signification.

The flash in the pan was born in the 1950s with the 30-second TV commercial, which helped to fuel national fads such as the hula-hoop, and achieved its apogee in the 1970s, with Gary Dahl's Pet Rock. Yet the concept makes available a less narrowly historical problematic that both links it to other forms of short duration, such as the ephemeral, the disposable and the obsolete, while also exceeding their primarily temporal common denominator. The flash in the pan does not live by time alone. Its animate flicker recasts architecture as provisional object,

a concentration of turned-on *mises-en-scène* held together
less by the stabilities of function, structure and space
and more by fleeting *qualities* and live action. As a result,
forms engendered by the flash in the pan are hard to look
at directly and are almost impervious to the traditional
historical gaze. Henry-Russell Hitchcock, for example,
seemed to consider architectural colour to have been a
flash in the pan, peering from the perspective of 1932 at its
presence in the architecture of the turn of the century the
way someone today might look at a photo of themselves
wearing purple bell-bottoms in the 1970s, repulsed and
attracted at the same time. He argued the allure of colour
had been useful to modernism in attracting attention to
the new style, especially when used on exteriors, but only
for a short while. It had very quickly revealed itself as
too subject to passing fashion and complicit in the world
of promotion and advertising: 'If architecture is not to
resemble billboards, colour should be both technically and
psychologically permanent.' For Hitchcock colour lacked
both the durability and disinterestedness he required of
architecture, even though it was essential to both
modernism's genesis and the billboard-filled visual field
in relation to which architecture was perceived.[18]

While Hitchcock's musings on colour seem to reveal
a begrudging appreciation for the flash in the pan, even
if he ultimately retained the preference for permanence
befitting a dean of modernism, Paul Rudolph's more
tenuous position as Dean of the Yale School of Architecture
in the waning days of modern architecture seems to
have inspired him to fully embrace the logic of the flash.
To say that Rudolph had a weakness for fads would be an
understatement. His New York apartment, which he
did not so much design – in the sense of giving it a final
architectural state – as continually redecorate until he
died, was famously stuffed with the newest materials of the
time, everything from shag carpet to Plexiglas and Mylar.
Visitors were bewildered by the faddish nature of his
domestic material palette and the flickering visual effects it
produced, and found it hard to remember these ambiences

in detail: Rudolph's interiors disappeared for decades in a blinding flash in the pan. On the other hand his drawings of these interiors, and of his own apartment in particular, were never forgotten, their astonishing demonstration of expertise in arguably the essential disciplinary technique permitting them to function as an unacknowledged point of contact between the logic of the flash and that of architecture as such. His drawings, in fact, demonstrate that the flash in the pan not only transforms the reception of architecture, but subverts its core disciplinary operations as well.

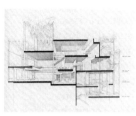

Section of Paul Rudolph
Apartment, 1967

Rudolph's ideation of space also exceeded the conventional limits of architectural representation.[19] To compensate, he developed a highly elaborated rendering technique, charged with an almost manic attention to detail. The large-scale renderings he favoured were often produced collectively and innovatively, employing mixed media including photographs and xeroxing. The resulting images display an almost blinding level of visual detail, indeed, Rudolph explained that he made them because 'the owner's insatiable desire to "see what the building looks like" must be satisfied'.[20] Yet his excessive investment in these renderings is not fully explained by such a banal rationale; he made such renderings even when there was no client, for example in his own apartment. But the most symptomatic aspect of Rudolph's relation to these drawings is revealed when he places the owner's insatiable desire to see what the building *looks like* in the present tense. The drawings in fact have little anticipatory value; they are better understood as compensation for the fact that the building – even when built – cannot be easily seen.

Ironically, however, the renderings, which are crowded with quasi-photographic detail, implacably reveal nothing at all about this interior. They make no effort to approximate the actual conditions anticipated in the structure either in terms of spatial experience or visual character. First, all Rudolph's significant drawings are sectional perspectives. This is an oddly hybrid form, since the section is normally used to show real spatial relationships while a perspective distorts real space in favour of a more fulsome illusion of spatiality. Rudolph's images thus superimpose two interiors – they show the interior squared. He consistently exacerbates this multiplicity by locating the perspectival vanishing point not at ground level, where one typically finds it in architectural renderings, but in the middle of his drawings, with spaces above and below. The intensified interior is thus suspended on the page, disconnected from the exterior, almost like a stage on which Rudolph performs the interiority of his designs.

This performance was strategically limited in scope. As Rudolph himself said, the rendering is 'fixed and ideal and completely unlike the building'. It does not indicate 'reflections or light and shadow or atmospheric or climatic conditions'.[21] While the drawings are in grisaille, they exclude chiaroscuro or sfumato, those atmospheric techniques that might have provided the graphic equivalent to the overpowering qualities of his spaces' décor. In this way, the drawings never represent what Rudolph called the different 'moods' of his buildings, showing only architectural and not psychological interiority. Indeed, the drawings are resolutely architectural, even excessively architectural: if drawing is a defining architectural operation and its medium is the line, then the dizzying number of lines in a Rudolph drawing allows the drawing itself, rather than the mood it represents, to produce a specifically disciplinary flash in the pan.

The Rudolph interior is thus doubly invisible: seen as a drawing it represents nothing, while experienced as a décor it is blinding. Moreover, and like a D'Arcy *mise-en-scène*, Rudolph's flashes in the pan were also an architecture turned on. In a Rudolph interior, flash made domesticity a pretence and a spectacle, requiring that the subject always be 'on', turning inhabitation into a performance and transfiguring inhabitants into domestic stars: the décor grants anyone 15 minutes of fame. Appropriately enough, parties that took place in interiors designed by Rudolph not only attracted Andy Warhol himself but garnered write-ups in the *New Yorker's* 'Talk of the Town'.[22]

Becoming the talk of the town is an important feature of the flash in the pan, which, amongst other things, is often recognised and disseminated by the buzz that surrounds it. The Rudolph interiors, like the D'Arcy displays or the *House Beautiful* projections – or, in a different sense, the spectacular media experiments of Gruppo 9999 and Environmental Communications – are conversation pieces to be talked about and settings for conversation over cocktails, their décor the formal analogue to the clink and clatter of drinks and chatter, full of background noise but no subtext, animated by talk but no consistent story, intimate but impersonal. The sociable performativity at stake in the space of the turn-on no longer tracks in the traditional architectural terms of public and private, but rather unfolds and is engendered in terms of duration and flash. Here the self is not a starting point but rather an effect, the net result of the *mises-en-scène*, while the formal and material conditions that emerge are those of the provisional object – unmemorable and atmospheric yet blinding. Banham's turn-on, D'Arcy's showrooms, turned-on décor, Gruppo's 9999 projections, EC's media frenzies and Rudolph's blinding interiors are all briefly evocative rather than memorable, spectacular rather than optical, effective rather than signifying. In other words, these flashes in the pan are flickering apparitions that, as the editors of *Domus* claimed, captivate only the corner of the eye, yet reveal where 'perhaps the new image of man was caught … between one flash and another'.[23]

FLASH IN THE PAN

NOTES

1. Reyner Banham, 'The Style: 'Flimsy … Effeminate?' in Mary Banham and Bevis Hillier (eds), *A Tonic to the Nation: The Festival of Britain* (London: Thames & Hudson, 1976), 196. For a broader discussion of Banham's comments on the festival, see Nigel Whitely, *Reyner Banham: Historian of the Immediate Future* (Cambridge, MA: MIT Press, 2003), 13ff.

2. There is by now a massive literature on the festival. A few titles that contain an architectural or design emphasis include Harriet Atkinson and Mary Banham, *The Festival of Britain: A Land and its People* (London: IB Tauris & Co, 2012); E Harwood and A Powers (eds), *Festival of Britain: Twentieth Century* 5 (London: Twentieth Century Society, 2001); and Becky Conekin, *The Autobiography of a Nation: The 1951 Festival of Britain* (Manchester: Manchester University Press, 2003).

3. Cited in 'Festival of Britain +10' in *Design*, May 1961, 51, 42.

4. See Kevin Lynch, *The Image of the City* (Cambridge, MA: MIT Press, 1960).

5. Except for the occasional mention, for example in Martin Filler's 'Rooms without People: Notes on the Development of the Model Room', *Design Quarterly* 109 (1979), 4–15 or in Marvin Traub's *Like No Other Store: The Bloomingdale's Legend and the Revolution in American Marketing* (New York: Times Books, 1993), there is very little literature on D'Arcy, who died in May 2012.

6. See Rita Reif, 'Will the Crowds Still Come to Look at the Model Rooms?', The *New York Times*, 2 February 1973.

7. See D'Arcy's introduction in her *Bloomingdale's Book of Home Decorating* (New York: Harper and Row, 1973).

8. The Gehry archive contains drawings of pieces of furniture made for this room, notably a large bed, but it does not contain drawings that describe the total environment, suggesting a collaboration between his office and hers.

9. One of the few historical theoretical statements made about this development is the *Discours préliminaire*, in C Percier and PFL Fontaine's *Recueil de décorations intériueres, compenant tout ce qui a rapport à l'ameublement…* (Paris, 1812).

10. For an introduction to Simmel's theory of sociability, see George Ritzer, *Modern Sociological Theory* (New York: McGraw-Hill, 2007), 158ff.

11. See 'Instant Interiors', *Progressive Architecture*, 48:6 (June 1967), 176–181 and 'Projection: The New Turned-On Décor', *House Beautiful* 109:9 (1967), 130–132.

12. The British equivalent to this phenomenon was referred to as 'switched on'. See Nigel Whiteley, 'Toward a Throw-Away Culture: Consumerism, "Style Obsolescence" and Cultural Theory in the 1950s and 1960s' in *Oxford Art Journal* 10:2, 'The 60s' 1987, 3–27.

13. This phenomenon can be easily tracked, for example in *Progressive Architecture*, where in June 1967 they published a piece called 'Instant Interiors' which featured, amongst other examples, the apartment of C Ray Smith, himself originally a theatre critic and at the time working to finish his book *Supermannerism*, where he took up the theme further. Shortly thereafter, in March 1968, *Progressive Architecture* then

ran an article entitled 'Instant Exteriors,' that described a happening made of images projected on freeway soffits and industrial silos orchestrated by Doug Michels (before forming Ant Farm) with Bob Field, as a protest against what they called city beautifiers in Washington DC. See the essay 'Supercharged' above.

14. See Gruppo 9999, 'Happening Progettuale' and 'Las Vegas' in *Casabella*, Aug/Sept 1969, 98–104 (the name of the group is incorrectly given as Gruppo 1999). The group had no particular leader and its members included M Preti, P Coggiola, A Gigli, C Caldini, G Sani and P Galli. Its work of this period is best documented in a self-published, limited edition book, *Ricordi di Architettura* (Florence, 1972).

15. Reyner Banham, *Architecture of the Well-Tempered Environment*, (Chicago: University of Chicago Press, 1969).

16. There is no scholarly literature on Environmental Communications available, save a few remarks in my *Everything Loose Will Land: 1970s Art and Architecture in Los Angeles* (Los Angeles and Vienna, 2013), 202ff, and 264.

17. *Domus* was describing the boutique *Altre Cose* in Milan by Ugo La Pietra. See 'Un architetto per vestire la moda: La boutique "Altre Cose" a Milano,' *Domus* 460 (March 1968), 32–37.

18. See Henry-Russell Hitchcock and Philip Johnson, *The International Style* (New York: Norton, 1997), 87.

19. While this aspect of the drawings is not discussed, the best study of Rudolph's drawings is Timothy Rohan's 'Rendering the Surface: Paul Rudolph's Art and Architecture Building at Yale', *Grey Room* 1 (Autumn 2000), 84–107. Although

widely published in decorator and interior design magazines and despite growing scholarly interest, most of Rudolph's domestic interiors, such as the Elman and the Eldersheim Apartments in New York, remain unknown.

20. Rudolph discusses his own approach to drawing in the introduction to *Paul Rudolph: Architectural Drawings* (London: Lund Humphries, 1974).

21. Ibid.

22. See George WS Trow, The Talk of the Town, 'Three Gatherings', *The New Yorker*, 30 January 1971, 22.

23. The description is of Derossi's Altro Mondo club in Turin. See Tomasso Trini, 'Divertimentifici', *Domus* 458 (January 1968).

OCCASIONAL

KISSING ARCHITECTURE:
SUPER-DISCIPLINARITY AND
CONFOUNDING MEDIUMS (2009)

'The basic concept was not to try to destroy or be
provocative to the architecture, but to melt in. As if I would
kiss Taniguchi. Mmmmm…' (said with closed eyes and
elaborate flourish, a bright yellow down vest and a heavy
Swiss accent). When Pipilotti Rist thus described her
Pour Your Body Out video installation in the atrium of
the Museum of Modern Art, she was of course not talking
about actually kissing Yoshio Taniguchi, the architect of the
museum. He was long gone by the time Rist entered
the scene, as was the largely ridiculed and largely phallic
broken obelisk that once punctuated the centre of the
atrium. Rather she was describing how her work would
come into temporary contact with Taniguchi's, how her
moving images would brush up against his still volume,
her shifting colours would apply moist pressure to his
white walls, how sound-filled nipples would bud from
his flatness and how this 'big room', 7,354 cubic metres
of uselessness devoted to ritualised transcendence, would
get filled up by sensuous bodies pouring in and out. She
was speaking with the voice of a not-architect of how
a new medium – I'll call it Super Architecture – and a new
sensibility – post-feminist certainly, but more acutely
one of intense affect – would simply and with devastating
generosity slip itself on and over the old medium of
architecture and its even older sensibilities of authority
and autonomous intellection, thereby enveloping the
increasingly archaic figure of the architect in a new cultural
project. Her remarks are a starting point for reconsidering
disciplinarity, expertise and medium specificity in

architecture today, because her affective yet alien embrace marks a regime change that is happening without the confrontation or violence prescribed by the avant-garde or the endless accommodations of new practice, but through the gesture of a sweetly gentle and yet thoroughly devastating kiss.

A kiss has been many things in many places. In the seventeenth century, Martin von Kempe wrote over 1,000 pages on kissing. But even Kempe could never have imagined that kissing would serve as a theory of architecture. Yet the kiss offers to architecture – a field that in its traditional forms has been committed to permanence and mastery – not merely the obvious allure of sensuality but a set of qualities architecture has long resisted: ephemerality and consilience. However long or short a kiss, however socially constrained or erotically desiring, a kiss is the coming together of two similar but not identical surfaces – surfaces whose geometry softens and flexes when in contact, perhaps to deform, a performance of temporary singularities, a union of bedazzling convergence and identification for the duration of which separation is inconceivable yet inevitable. Kissing confounds the division between two bodies, pouring them together temporarily to create new definitions of boundary, loosening the fixity of form and structure and updating the metric of time. Further, one cannot speak when kissing and hence, while often charged with significance, kissing interrupts how faces and facades communicate, substituting affect and force for representation and meaning. Kissing is the end of faciality, a thought expressed by Andy Warhol's wry observation that 'two people kissing always look like fish'. And yet, as cold-blooded as fish may be, as alienating and deforming as kissing is, as divorced as this definition of it is from traditional notions of emotion and love and even death, kissing cannot be critical. A critical kiss is a bite and not a kiss, and hence bringing architecture and kissing together is not only to reconsider architecture's relation to other mediums but to think beyond prevailing models of the critical. Kissers, whether or not they actually like each other, inevitably lack precisely the separation needed for critical distance and opposition. Architecture has long served as a model of failure, disaster and complicity – now architecture really needs a kiss, to kiss, and a theory of kissing.

Before considering kissing in general, it's worth pausing for a moment to ask why Pipilotti Rist is kissing Taniguchi in particular and what it means, if anything, that this kiss took place at MoMA. The Museum of Modern Art has long considered itself to be the very home of good architectural design and remains the institution of record for architecture, using its exhibits and collections to constitute itself as the standard-bearer of value and importance, not only in the US but still for Europe as well. In other words, what happens at MoMA does not stay at MoMA but rather aspires to the status of disciplinarity as such. But the museum has consistently betrayed its obligation to architecture by constructing a series of buildings one more boring than the last. By the 1980s, the difference between the architecture of Deconstruction (1988), the apex of the critical turn, and the architecture of Cesar Pelli's mall (1984), the apex of capitalist capitulation, was stupefying. The most recent failure – Taniguchi's 1997 addition – was an expected but no less disappointing confirmation of MoMA's historic commitment to distinguishing between the progressive architecture in the museum (in its exhibitions, archives and public programmes) and the unspeakably banal architecture of the museum.

And yet banality is an integral part of why and how Rist's kiss operated architecturally. *Pour Your Body Out* inserted a super intense affective environment into an architectural volume that itself was nothing, barely even rising to the occasion of the generic or white box. Instead, the architecture of MoMA (and not just MoMA, but all architecture for which MoMA is not a scapegoat but a stand-in) is merely what you bump up against when you back up to look at some art, with neither an inside nor an outside, neither utopian nor existential, but rather perfectly and intentionally insipid. In fact, MoMA's architectural banality is the key means by which the museum has attempted to maintain its commitment to the modernist – in Clement Greenberg's terms the avant-garde – project and to establish and perpetuate that project's supposed universality. For Greenberg, the proof that the spirit of modernity was present was revealed when the viewer's response to an object was purely and laboriously cognitive without affect. All experience of intensity or immediacy betrayed, according to Greenberg, the presence of emotion that risked overcoming intellection and therefore risked turning art into kitsch. Insisting that architecture maintain such a profound lack of character without even a ghostly spectre of feeling is not a lack of position or accidental design flaw but rather a commitment to a once progressive and now painfully outmoded position struggling to maintain its faded hegemony.

The behaviour of visitors to MoMA reveals this outmodedness. The continuous movement of people, goods and images – from the street, where most visitors' time is spent waiting in line, to gallery floors, where no one ever actually stops since the intrinsically peripatetic museum-goer is, in the Taniguchi extension, rather an obstacle to be moved along by the non-space of circulation, and finally to the store – is not only a constant performance of the collapse of Greenberg's opposition between kitsch and the avant-garde but an index of the flow of affect and its effects on behaviour. In this case, the logic of the museum that separates the aesthetic realm from the commercial realm is undercut not just by the capital that operates in both but by the drive to compensate for the 'don't touch' distance demanded in the galleries by unleashing acquisitive desire in the store. Increasingly, museums are foreplay, appetite-whetters, creating excited visitors who can only consummate their aesthetic experience elsewhere. The museum is in fact an affect-producing machine, an ideal mechanism for a culture, as Brian Massumi has argued, which contains an excess of affect but a lack of places to put it and even less vocabulary with which to describe it.

Describing the effects of Rist kissing Taniguchi is a
first step in the development of a new vocabulary adequate
to the character of contemporary culture, because their
kiss was utterly impersonal, did not involve their bodies,
described no feelings of love and yet produced disciplinary
intimacy and material closeness. The viewer perceived
the heat of entanglement but read no love story. Their kiss
produced experience but did not describe their experience.
Our capacity to understand the aesthetic is still rooted in
Greenberg's association of affect with personal experience
or sentiment and hence the distinction of experience as
such is hard to grasp. But if affect is understood as the
internalisation of perception – and precisely not as personal
feelings shaped by symbolism, language and other forms
of cultural predeterminations – if we no longer need to
equate detachment and distance with intellection and
abstraction nor feeling with crude sentimentality, then we
can return to experience with new theoretical vigour. Rist's
kiss was neither a shock to the architectural system in
the tradition predicated on the detachment of the critical
avant-garde nor a reinforcement of the distinction between
architectural abstraction and kitsch, but a vivid moment –
the swerve itself – of intense affect in the otherwise opiated
milieu of MoMA.

The convergence of Rist and Taniguchi in MoMA
is an excuse for describing a series of contradictions
that characterise both the external environment in
which architecture is produced and the internal logic of
architectural thought itself. What *Pour Your Body Out* offers
to architecture is not dependent on the particular content of
Rist's work but rather on her medium's mode of operation
in relation to architecture. The installation provokes a
theory of surface founded in the touching of (at least) two
surfaces – surfaces that in their twoness bring either
material or epistemological difference, as opposed to the
standard form of thinking of surface as an abstract and
undifferentiated plane that functions above all to veil a
depth. Fredric Jameson theorised postmodernism as a play
of surfaces, but we have still not adequately (and literally)

fleshed out his theory to understand how surfaces interact with one another as material rather than representational entities. Once attended to through this more dense and haptic focus on the architectural surface, we can recognise the multiple ways in which it is stroked, encased, enveloped and consumed by the 'software' of media and other material furnishings. And we can accumulate these sensations until their erotic combinations render the kiss a potent technique for producing new affects: if tragedy was once considered the apex of artistic expression, let us say that the kiss is today's highest form of sensation, one that caresses the spectator to nudge aside the jaded gaze of the recent past and move towards new forms of acutely contemporary experience.

Because of its traditional role as what was called 'mother of the arts', architecture has generally been more able than most mediums to understand itself in relational terms. The common theme of these various understandings has been notions of the whole, from the baroque idea of the unity of the arts, to the nineteenth-century theory of the *gesamkunstwerk* to the modern idea of total design. More recently, for those like Peter Eisenman who are particularly revolted by being cast in the role of mother, architecture's relation to other mediums has been defined in terms of radical autonomy and specificity, whether material, technical or semantic. In other words, architecture's history of disciplinary embeddedness in culture is a history of all or nothing. But the Rist installation, in part because it works through projected and moving images, suggests that the seductive contact between architecture and not-architecture is a place to think inductively about how the capacities of one medium can mingle with and boost those of another with neither losing its specificity. For example, architecture has never been very good at speaking and at being an image, although it has and continues to desire imageability. But architecture is good at bearing images, especially when in the contact between image and surface there is neither autonomy nor mastery, but surplus, extra and often surprise, not quite uncanny but just unexpected added value, like a two for one. This is a model of consilience, of pouring things together that do not mix but cannot be separated, like pouring your body out and into MoMA, or having Pipilotti Rist kiss Taniguchi.

Kissing is a lot of things: classical, symbolic (the air kiss), political, *passé* and a marketing device. In the vocabulary of new soft urbanism buildings too are said to kiss. But for architecture today, it is most useful to think about kissing as an experience of contact between at least two surfaces that begins before language and culture. Kissing may begin with suckling, turn into grooming, continue as oral fixation, find sublimated means of expression and may ultimately become erotic. Kissing may be self-soothing and appeasing. But ultimately, in these terms, kissing becomes something you cannot satisfactorily

Pipilotti Rist, *Solution for Man Solution for Woman*, 2011, Wexner Center for the Arts

do alone. In kissing you seek another mouth that is like yours but is not yours. Kissing always involves the surprise of this difference. Kissing is not a collaboration between two that aims to make one unified thing, but is the intimate friction between two mediums to produce twoness. There is reciprocity but

not identity, and it is though reciprocity that kissing opens new epistemological and formal models for redefining architecture's relation to other mediums and hence to itself.

Luce Irigaray described the alteration to perception achieved by the kiss as its capacity to make the 'world grow so large that the horizon itself disappears'. And this indeed well describes one aspect of the perceptual effect of *Pour Your Body Out*: the proportions of the projections establish a horizon line that extends the atrium into the deep, perhaps even infinite space of the outside world. And yet at the same time the effect of the video on the perception of the atrium was to interiorise it: the projection cinched the inside of the room and gave it an enveloping and containing horizon line. The video took this indefinite space, which by itself is indeterminately circulation, gallery, destination, and gave it definition. All of the additional elements of the project reinforced this transformation of loose flow into dense accumulation: the sound system that made the wall surfaces protrude towards the centre, the pink curtains that discharged leakage into the rest of the museum, the carpet and pouf that established a floor and a centre, and the changed body position of the viewers who were now compelled ergonomically to look at the ceiling and who hence gave the room a top. With no permanent or significant material alteration to the constituent elements of the architecture's abstract universal space, the videos turned it into a bounded interior packed with sound and animation and poured up to the top with bodies. An oozy and ill-defined volume was compressed into a room susceptible to being filled with a density of effects that superseded opticality and frontality as the mode of address to the viewer and hence intensified synaesthetic affectation of the visitor. The atrium went from vapid to vivid. Architecture has a long and rich history of finding forms of compensation for its own incapacity to move, for its reliance on permanence and solidity. Indeed one of the fascinating perversions of the field has been the substitutes architecture has found for these qualities it lacks, from rustication to reflectivity, from serpentine form to inflatable structure. Yet architecture might, like a child who sucks his thumb and attempts to seek substitutes in its own body for the virtual and the animate, sooner or later find this inadequate. The thumb doesn't kiss back and the skin does not have what has been called the sensory and muscular virtuosity of the mouth. To kiss yourself contains no surprise and no new sensations. But when architecture abandons its fantasy of establishing models of organic unity and allows the interior distinction and detachment, it discovers the pleasures and possibilities of the kiss: kissing takes two and it is only when and if the interior is understood as not-architecture that it can stand in relation to architecture as if a kiss. The interior is quasi-autonomous – it relies on and is even often isomorphic with architecture, but remains distinct from architecture's identification with building. As a result, the interior is uniquely free to seek out provisionality and changefulness and to provide architecture with a site of experimentation. The interior coordinates surfaces that are in sufficient proximity with one another that they amplify each other's effects. In its relation to architecture, the interior establishes not an expanded field (as Rosalind Krauss called it) but rather a densifying vortex of visually reverberating vertical surfaces. When contact between surfaces is deployed to conjure an interior ambience that is not architecture, but just millimetres shy of architecture proper, the psychologically intimate and physiologically momentary nature of the interior surprises a stolid and solid architecture as if with a kiss.

What contemporary visual practices are discovering in the dense laminates of the interior are the effects of confounding architecture, of pouring mediums together in ways that generate the bedazzling states of difference and identity embedded in a kiss. This discovery is pushing architecture to overcome its disciplinary disappointment at its failure to be totally self-sustaining and to relinquish its fantasy of absolute autonomy and domination. What is interesting about the possibilities open to architecture today is that it is finding more gratifying forms of what it has sought again and again. When Rist kisses Taniguchi, architecture itself is surprised into responding, made aware of the added value of another's mouth seeking neither nourishment nor reproduction. So kissing architecture requires not only that architecture receive the kiss, but that it participate in return: that it kiss back. In other words, the reciprocity of kissing offers not just an analysis of how a particular video installation altered a particular work of architecture but of how mediums today might interact. Media theory would suggest that if superarchitecture is an emerging supermedium, a minimum of two mediums or epistemologically distinct surfaces intimate content, the impact of the medium rather than its content. Consider what McLuhan said about the telephone: 'Why should the phone create an intense feeling of loneliness? ... Why does a phone ringing ... create instant tension? ... The answer to all of these questions is simply that the phone is a participant form that demands a partner, with all the intensity of electric polarity.' Rist's intervention rang architecture's bell, and persuaded it – even if against its will in the case of Taniguchi – to perform through borrowed qualities, such as movement, colour, narrative and sound. In responding, architecture became not merely visible, as Marshall McLuhan understood the effect of new mediums on old mediums, but eidetic – not just visible but vivid. Kisses make architecture pick up the phone and participate in intense and intimate moments of affect. And since architecture has had the unique privilege and responsibility of housing the one and representing the many, recalibrating how architecture extends itself, how its one gently shifts the limits of the other to create provisional if profound pressure between two, rather than a utopian collapse into unity, is to redesign how architecture exercises power and diagrams politics. As a result, kissing architecture is not a private matter, but an urgent call to ethical action.

First published in *Log* 17 (2010)

THE RAW AND THE COOKED (2011)

Futuristic computer animations and eschatological
predictions of impending ecological doom to the
contrary, architecture is in the midst of a widespread
return to what eighteenth-century theorists would have
called first principles. In combination with reports that
find buildings responsible for no less than 50 per cent of
worldwide energy consumption, making them significant
contributors to the acute crises brought about by climate
change, the latest digital tools have encouraged the
view that architecture today occupies a unique historical
position in relation to both technology and nature.
Yet a resurging deployment of geometric primitives,
appeals to the laws of ecology and, perhaps most of all,
a renewed desire to claim for architecture the capacity to
shape a universal mind through embodied experience,
all make contemporary architectural discourse
uncannily reminiscent of the arguments of figures such
as Quatremère de Quincy, Cuvier and Condillac. These
historical resonances reveal that, rather than being
radically contemporary and separated into two camps –
those who would subsume disciplinary questions in
favour of sustainability advocacy and those who see
no link between the coincident reappearance of organic
form and the global alarm about natural resources – the
list of issues that preoccupy architects today betrays
a fundamental attachment to an almost Rousseauian
world view: his state of nature may now be today's tribal
chic, but both look to the possibility of the unmediated,
to the thing outside the vagaries of culture, in the hope
that such a state of rawness might make possible a new
form of synthetic agency and a radical reconstitution
of architecture's horizons.

In seeking to understand the surprising historical connection between eighteenth-century and current naturalisms, it is useful to recall that the culmination of Enlightenment thinking did not take place until some 200 years after Rousseau. By then, it was possible for anthropologist Claude Lévi-Strauss to argue that the opposition between the raw and the cooked was an organising principle of culture in all times and in all places. His structuralist approach, rooted in the notion that culture obeys universal laws that can be scientifically explained, was fully articulated in the work considered by many to be his most important, *Mythologiques*, of which *The Raw and the Cooked* is the first volume.[1] One of his most profound achievements in this text was to transform, with minimalist elegance, the morass of theories attempting to chart the evolution of the natural into the cultural into a simple straight line diagramming the opposition between the one and the other, with man himself as mediator. Today, the economies and the confidences that underpinned this schema – which relied on the notion of a universal subject and had not yet fully imagined how genetic engineering, to give just one example, would undermine the capacity to distinguish between the natural and the cultural – have long since given way to an emphasis on the continuities between these states. The traces of Lévi-Strauss's opposition sometimes remain at work, however, in the thinking of those who seem most devoted to its undoing. As a result, the vicissitudes of the raw and cooked are a surprisingly useful barometer of contemporary architectural commitments.[2]

Although present with ever-diminishing vigour since the eighteenth century cooked up a hut from raw trees and timber, natural themes were almost totally expunged from architecture by the discipline's linguistic turn in the 1970s. In fact, what ultimately became the architectural theory of the 1990s was predicated on the total eradication from the discourse of questions of materials, phenomenology and other naturalisms. Yet a quick survey of the contemporary field reveals that an initially tentative reintroduction of natural themes has picked up speed and changed its character. At first, 'nature' paradoxically re-entered the architectural scene through the mechanisms of the theory that had at first exiled it: the poststructuralism that entered the field from literary circles in the 1980s became by the 1990s a vector for the engagement of architecture with chaos theory, borrowed from mathematical circles. Their conjunction would provoke increasing interest in calculus, topology and, eventually, that ground zero of theorisations of nature, fractal geometry. Indeed, undoubtedly not for their truth value but simply because fractals and complexity already appeared so architectural (or at least relied on visualisation protocols that were easy to translate into architecture), these schema became an opportunity to unleash the long repressed naturalist impulse in architecture. By the late 1990s the philosophical implications of poststructuralist reconsiderations of nature were often reduced to a pictorial platitude and resulted in design studios filled with buildings shaped like trees or mountains. Ironically, these banal proposals were largely insulated from criticism by the very naturalness of their appearance – who wants to censure nature itself? But even if the representation of weather systems and butterfly effects in particular proved to be a dead-end, they played a role in initiating a broader shift in focus from abstract systems to concrete material life that turns out to have been the beginning of a still unfolding effort by architecture to uncook its books, to reassemble itself from raw elements and fundamentals (whether conceived of as natural resources or as-found shapes): they forecasted a more pervasive drama of architecture 'going native'.[3]

There are too many steps to recount between the first signs of love for self-determining natural systems, from fractals to slime moulds, that fascinated architects for almost two decades and the current marriage of professional organisations such as the NAAB and the AIA to the complex ideology of sustainability. But a trail from 'nature' as element of cultural analysis to 'nature' as signifying system (and, frequently, moral code mandating professional standards) is nevertheless evident. The craze for Mandelbrot's groovy scaling shapes was quickly tempered by the coy phenomenology of Herzog & de Meuron, the artificial weather stations of Olafur Eliasson and the natural histories given to landform buildings. There could have been nothing more unnatural than the cloud of the Blur building, except perhaps the Frank Gehry and Greg Lynn project for a resort on Sentosa Island in Singapore organised around a zoo for exotic sea animals, which the two designers filled with giant robotic creatures to produce a show that hovered ambiguously between a display of paleolithic specimens and an Archigram-like spectacle of moving buildings. From a perspective within the field, these projects have little in common. From a broader perspective, however, these projects are evidence of a disciplinary struggle to transform architecture from its status in the 1990s as text and representation into an articulate and forceful agent in the material world.

Further examples abound: within the last decade, Los Angeles-based architect Jason Payne, increasingly known as a materialist provocateur, conducted a studio in which students were asked to design projects entirely from cow rawhides bought via the internet; for one of its Young Architects Program projects, MoMA filled the PS1 courtyard with farm animals; and François Roche and Philippe Parreno have been powering a building in Thailand with elephant shit. And in the meantime, professional practice has been expanding its market share with corporate buildings that breathe fresh air, are covered with plants and reduce carbon footprints, all the while engaging in its own struggle for agency in the world of capital and power. At no time in the recent past has the conflict between the discipline and the profession been more acute: their two realities – in which the profession claims architecture can solve 'real problems' (now ecological more than social), while the discipline claims to use architecture to question the status of the real itself – are stretched across a seemingly enormous divide.

But going native is precisely the one thing that crosses this divide. Underlying both approaches, no matter how seemingly divergent, is a desire for rawness and a conviction that the raw is no longer merely opposed to the cooked, but the dominant term in the binary. Going native, in fact, is increasingly the common denominator of a vast range of contemporary cultural trends, everything from celebrity philanthropy to the policy of the EPA to the flows of global capital. Indeed, this inversion of modernity's traditional temperament – which saw the cooked as inexorably replacing the raw – is nowhere more evident than in the current resonance between our cultures of food and architecture. They have a long history of entanglement, from the corn motifs carved onto ancient capitals to Enlightenment theories of taste and *le bon gout*, which provided a common ground for the appreciation of all things aesthetic, from the culinary to the visual to the tectonic. But today, beyond these historic associations, food and architecture share a fundamental embeddedness in a particular combination of matters of survival, pleasure and production that allows them to serve as uniquely useful gauges of contemporary cultural structures.

For example, it was not so long ago that elBulli, the Catalan restaurant run by chef Ferran Adrià and famous as a hotspot of molecular gastronomy, the most scientifically concocted of cuisines, rose to the top of the food chain to become widely understood as one of the great cultural achievements of the late twentieth century. At elBulli, the preparation of food, which was traditionally the primary means of intercourse between the cultural and the natural – the moment of transformation from raw to cooked – became instead a means to use carbon dioxide, nitrogen and centrifuges to spin every last natural molecule out of consumption. Tomatoes were transformed into the essence of tomato, a rosy piece of air with neither nutritional value nor taste, a pure exercise in culinary abstraction. While elBulli is now closed, the slow food movement, which seeks to resist the globalisation of fast food by relinking gastronomy to local ecosystems, has burgeoned. That movement may have slowed food down, but it is ultimately the raw food movement or rawism, which espouses a diet of uncooked, unpasteurised and unprocessed food, that reveals the gastronomic trajectory of the twenty-first century is not only returning towards Rousseau's relatively bucolic state of nature, but heading far beyond it, into a wild blue yonder.

Meanwhile, architecture is working hard to discover what its own state of nature might be. There are many different flavours of raw architecture operating today – whether we understand cooking in relation to carbon footprints, building refuse, naturalising forms, or the solicitation of unmediated forms of perception – but two have emerged as primary. The first category is the neo-primitivist, which includes such diverse things as rough-hewn materials, affinities for base affects, and a decidedly not anthropological interest in substandard housing from Mumbai to Brazil. The second category is the ecological, which also ranges widely from interest in environmental control systems, to toxic land reclamation, to the neurobiol-ogy of architectural experience. Yet none of these varieties recognise each other as kin, and indeed, how less related could LEED certification and a rawhide studio seem to be? The refusal to acknowledge fraternity is a necessary condition of the commitment to the raw: recognition that there might be two ways not to cook a building would betray the constructed – rather than natural – nature of all 'raw' architecture as a category. Rawness in architecture can only be staged, since never under any circumstances could any kind of architecture be produced outside the operations of culture. Architecture is by definition cooked.

That architecture's current appeal to nature is intrinsically rhetorical does not lessen its importance, although it should dispense with discussions about its truth-value and redirect critical attention precisely to its rhetoric. In fact, while the many appeals appear to be made on behalf of the most current conditions, both of architecture's primary naturalising rubrics are best understood as a contemporary unfolding of the long tradition of one of rhetorical theory's principal figures, imitation: mimesis is back. The single most persistent theme in the visual arts in the west since antiquity – the tenet that made art artful and cooked as opposed to a raw material – was its imitation of nature.[4] Mimesis management was the one skill shared by every artist and architect from Phideas to Frank Lloyd Wright. Yet this perennial attachment to mimesis has been marked by an often vituperative disagreement about how to effect the imitation. Although it stemmed from an antique philosophical dispute about the nature of Divine creation, Alberti codified this conflict as a core element of art and architectural theory in the fifteenth century, when he expressed it as the distinction between *natura naturata* and *natura naturans*. The first principle defined art in terms of its capacity to interpret nature and to produce works that most closely represented nature and its forces. This notion made the visual arts autonomous from the dictates of ideality, for example permitting Leonardo to draw grotesques and everyone from Caravaggio to Van Gogh to Warhol to select dirty or poorly shod feet as a legitimate subject matter for works of art. The second principle was, on the other hand, a more active argument that art could operate in the manner – rather than the image – of nature, harnessing natural forces and even improving on natural phenomena. *Natura naturans* thus freed artists from the 'as found,' making it possible to understand things not existing in nature as natural: the most famous application of this principle was the common Renaissance technique of selecting a nose from this figure, a toe from that one, a torso from the other, and putting them together to create an even better subject than could be fashioned by nature itself.

The fundamental distinction between *natura naturata* and *natura naturans* remains in force in the dissention between current neo-primitivist and ecological paradigms. The neo-primitives share with Leonardo a quest for points of departure that are within nature but outside traditional conventions of beauty or ideal states of matter. The continuity between the primitive hut and the geometric

primitives that abound in computer-aided design and
parametric discourse is not generally recognised, but

both have been constituted by
architecture as 'natural' (ie
'original') objects from which
variations can be derived. In this
way, everything from log cabins
to deformed squares are used as a
means to produce unprecedented
interpretations of nature, to
discover subnatures, and to
expand the range of natures
considered worthy of imitation.

Jason Payne,
Raspberry Fields, 2009–10

The ecologists, on the other hand, are more idealist and
hence more driven by abstraction. They produce landform
buildings (so large and complex that they function
as ecologies in their own right), epigenetic landscapes, or
use multiple species as models for architecture to intellect
natures that do not – and could never – exist.

Both strategies have their strengths and their pitfalls.
The benefit for the neo-primitivists derives from what
they might call encouraging greater diversity in their
genetic pool: shifting from platonic forms to Moebius strips
evidently expands architecture's geometric (and hence
organisational) range. On the other hand the risk of
neo-primitivist rhetoric lies in defining objects as within
nature because they fall outside particular social and
political conventions. For example, the transformation
of the ad-hoc urbanism of Lagos into the 'natural' basis
of the designed urbanism of OMA turns neo-primitivism
back into old school primitivism – an Africanist version
of Said's *Orientalism*.[5] While the divide of colonial power
is no longer that between east and west, defining anything
within a state of this kind of nature remains the first step
towards its colonisation and subjugation. The more absolute
primitivism becomes, the more it corrupts absolutely.

The ecologists have good resource husbandry
intentions on their side but risk reproducing well-worn
essentialising arguments in artificial terms (a common

by-product of morally based arguments). Suggesting that architects should model environmental experience on the visceral response to being in a tree on the savannah surrounded by predatory animals, as one critic has recently done, may be intended to provoke an awareness of what founders of the modern environmental movement like Barry Commoner called the connectedness of things, but it inadequately accounts for the many different ways you might find yourself in such a tree: because you are a bird, because you are on a first-class safari, or because you are out rustling up some dinner. While ecology helps us understand ourselves as part of the animal kingdom, our perceptions inevitably pass through culture on their way to consciousness, and that culture is neither colour- nor class- nor species-blind.

Neither strategy, however, can escape an essentially mimetic orientation. Though ecologists criticise neo-primitivists for being principally concerned with represen-tational issues (focusing on the appearances rather than the procedures of nature), they have their own system for replicating natural systems. Some proponents of the latter favour scripts and parametrics, and while coders claim innocence, it is not by a process of natural selection that the forms generated by their programmes look, well, organic. Shifting the object of mimesis from a natural object to a natural force is a change in degree rather than in kind. Ironically, some ecologists also claim for themselves a more active role in environmental management, because they deal with 'real' data derived directly from the metrics of sustainable energy or material use, but the neo-primitivists may be better at causing the ideological realignments necessary for any substantive transformation in environmental policy.

Picking sides in this debate is not a question of nature or even of architecture, but is rather an ethical matter. Historically speaking, many an evil thing justified its will to power by recourse to the authority of natural law. Most of today's architectural naturalists were trained by yesterday's historian/theorists, so one can be quite sure that the current inattention to the historical record cannot be caused by simple ignorance but must be a manifestation of a repression or even a deliberate erasure of a troublesome lineage. The attractions of sustainability, which often include its use as a marketing device, are luring architects to use rhetoric that relies more and more on what is now – or again – assumed to be the absolute value and authority of nature, invoked as a means of privileging one form of practice over another. Gilles Deleuze was famously suspicious of arguments that began with the word 'I', because he believed that the invocation of personal experience was the first step towards an inevitable privileging of the self;[6] he found the logic of the first person to be intrinsically reactionary. A similar critique could be levelled against the way many architects now deploy nature to foreclose other options and privilege an often unintellected position, smuggling reactionary thinking into the discipline in the guise of the unimpeachably natural.

These problems are nowhere clearer than in contemporary attitudes towards materials. No one still believes in the modernist ideal of the 'nature of materials.' Or do they? Today we probably wouldn't ask a brick what it wants to be, but prevailing cultural trends suggest that most would agree that using a brick for a second time, any brick in any fashion, is a good thing. Recycling is the new material nature enabling the architect not only to mobilise the discourses of sustainability but to project onto matter a protean capacity for endless transformation and regeneration. Recycling helps the architect act as Lévi-Strauss's trickster, the agent who is able to cross between the cooked and the raw or, in this architectural context, to return something from the realm of cooked to a state of nature, allowing it to re-enter the cycle of production and consumption in the guise of something raw. This almost mythical transformation can be generative for the architectural discipline, but the evidence that large corporate offices are getting larger and fatter by 'going green' also indicates the need to be attentive to the significant divide between the way architecture as a profession engages with matters like recycling and the way architecture as a discipline understands such questions.

In an ideal world, these two dimensions of architecture would of course converge – and that is certainly the purported goal of New Practice – but in this less than ideal world recycling in architecture risks becoming just another capitalist gambit to make money out of waste. So before mounting a full-scale effort to calibrate the architectural contribution to environmental management by counting up piles of building waste or the number of recycled materials used in an office tower, it would be interesting to examine the accounting ledgers of architectural firms and their principals to see how much money they donate to the Sierra Club, Greenpeace or other organisations who have a disciplinary mandate to solve environmental issues. Chances are good that such an exercise would demonstrate that architecture – understood as an economic venture – has no less but certainly no more purchase on environmental improvement than dentistry, rocket science or any other profession.

Sustainability represents the latest in a long chain of pseudo-ameliorations through which architecture has demonstrated time and again that it is a weak player in the world of global capital. Today, architecture should spend its resources elsewhere. Indeed, it is a field equipped to catalyse the remediation (rather than return) that will be necessary to achieve a contemporary version of Rousseau's state of nature by doing what it does best: asking probing questions about the nature of artificial environments, and determining which aspects of these environments are worth preserving or reusing, which kinds of reuse are tolerable and which are not and, finally, which kinds of materials can successfully cycle through the states of nature, production, overproduction and abjection until they are once more available as raw agents. Recycling will never work as an ecological diagram if the goal is to take the cooked and make it raw: it is the quest for rawness itself, for a state of nature (even if artificially manufactured) along with all the elements of purity, control and virtue such a state implies, that is intrinsically futile and contra-ecological. Instead, by looking at the vicissitudes of the raw and the cooked, by recalibrating the values attached to materials as such, by reconsidering how much is enough, by asking if waste is just a good thing in the wrong place, architecture can be a strong ally of substantive environmental thinking and a potent opponent of regressive ideologies that propagate an opposition between the raw and the cooked. The new mimesis underlying architecture's desire to go native need not signal the end of architecture as a cultural practice, as long as we understand that it manifests no natural laws and carries no absolute weight. Instead, it is by reopening long-running arguments about mimesis that we can sharpen architecture's understanding of the multiple natures it generates, and it is these debates in turn that will sustain our field.

First published in Preston Scott Cohen and Erika Naginski (eds), *The Return of Nature: Sustaining Architecture in the Face of Sustainability* (London: Routledge, 2014).

NOTES

1. Claude Lévi-Strauss, *The Raw and the Cooked: Mythologiques* vol I, trans John Weightman and Doreen Weightman (Chicago: University of Chicago Press, 1983)

2. These thematics were taken up in the exhibition *The Raw and the Cooked*, curated by Dan Cameron and held at the Reina Sofia Centre, Madrid, 1994.

3. See the discussion of going native in Bill Ashcroft (ed), *Key Concepts in Post-Colonial Studies* (London: Routledge, 1998).

4. As befits the subject, there is a massive literature on mimesis. Two good points of departure for this discussion include Rensselaer W Lee, *Ut Pictura Poesis, The Humanistic Theory of Painting* (New York: WW Norton & Co, 1967) and Anthony Blunt, *Artistic Theory in Italy 1450–1600* (Oxford: Oxford University Press, 1985).

5. Edward Said, *Orientalism* (New York: Vintage Books, 1979).

6. See Gilles Deleuze, *Negotiations* (New York: Columbia University Press, 1997), 11–12.

KEEPING UP WITH
THE ARCHITECTS (2011)

Despite popular opinion, feelings are not transhistorical
phenomena, common to all people at all times. They emerge
and evolve prompted by the constant reconfigurations of
the infinite number of forces that shape affective life.
New feelings, as a result, are useful distinguishing markers
for understanding the complexion of these forces: their
geometry, direction and power. The particular flavour
of envy that architecture feels for certain types of media,
especially their apparently greater currency and
consequence, is one such response that perfectly and
impersonally gives evidence to the technological and
spatial underpinnings of contemporary subjectivity.
Of course the general category of envy, with its range of
expressions from competitive rage to petty resentments,
is historically familiar. But architecture's regard for media,
touched as it is with lust and loathing in unequal measure,
and marked above all by architecture's frustrated sense
of lagging behind, is a comparatively recent phenomenon.
And this is not only because the media in question,
from TV to video games, are themselves relatively new,
but because the emergence of the feeling required that
the suburbs establish themselves, conceptually, as the
new ground of life.

The idiom that best encapsulates the feeling state
generated by the convergence of architecture with
media is the desire to keep up with the Joneses. While a
commonplace emotion, it is also importantly an inherently
architectural affect produced specifically by the suburban
regime. The wish that your house were bigger than
your neighbour's, the jealousy that they were the first on

the block to have an Xbox Kinect, reflects a precise type of desire that could only be born of the particular alchemy produced by suburbia. It requires the combination of closeness, independence, social mobility, acquisitiveness and the promise of equality and fairness that is the bedrock of suburban order. Sameness has to be represented for difference to be so keenly felt.

Identity and repetition are, of course, key elements in the architectural and planning logic of suburbia, generated by the procedures of mass production and realised through the replication of basic housing types and architectural details, with regulatory design codes controlling outdoor spaces and sameness in the layout of streets and services. But what is important in this context is the fact that this structure of repetition generated, and was revealed through, small acts of variation – variation that in turn provoked piques and resentments large and small. This affective by-product of suburban architecture was particularly acute in the curatorial cadence of the homeowner. Possessions were notoriously displayed in such a way – through picture windows, on front driveways, in backyards demarcated by neighbourly and hence not overly imposing fences – that constant and irritating comparison became inevitable. If maintaining the fictional democracy of the suburbs required the belief that possessions rather than birth had become the metric of the social order, this order was lubricated just enough by the norms of exhibiting property to allow slippage from one side of the class divide to the other. Borrowing someone's lawnmower, generally left on display through an open garage door, became a momentary foray into another's identity. Suburbia so pursued this logic of proximity, identity and visibility that the drama of neighbourly relations became more important than the performers themselves. Revealingly, in the cartoon strip that gave birth to the expression 'keeping up with the Joneses', the neighbours were never actually drawn. Instead their implicit adjacency provided enough of a *frisson* enough to keep the series interesting for almost 30 years.[1]

Architecture and media have a suburban rapport. This is not only because the suburb was where architecture and a whole panoply of media became entangled, the duet between the television screen and the picture window being the best-known example of the veritable isomorphism of postwar building and media. The rapport is suburban because it generates the affective order of 'keeping up with the Joneses'. From the moment it noticed media had moved in next door, architecture has felt itself to be in a constant race to keep up with a neighbour annoyingly close, too close to ignore, but too fast and agile to be caught. Condescendingly rejecting the suburban regime at every opportunity, architecture nevertheless adopted its promise of parity and sameness, converting the promise into the use of media as the standard and measure of architectural value. Architecture wanted to keep up with, to be the same as, to be equal to media. By the 1960s, using media became the primary attribute of what made advanced architecture advanced until, in the writings of Reyner Banham most notably, but with many other critics as well, architecture was not only reclassified according to the categories of software and hardware but encouraged to give up its hardness altogether in order to become like media. Having once wished for status of alpha dog in the pack of cultural production, architectural drive was transformed by the suburban order into the will to be the perpetual beta.

If *Keeping Up with the Kardashians* is any indication, new feelings can become newer still; if in cartoon form the neighbours were never visible, in reality TV the spectacle of the neighbours has utterly taken over. But even if we now leer at the neighbours as much as at their possessions – the cameras making possible this voyeurism and the domestic intimacies it purportedly offers – suburbia remains the matrix for an emerging reconfiguration of the neighbourly manners of architecture and media. A powerful and recent piece of evidence in support of this fact is *The Suburbs*, the 2010 award-winning CD of the Montreal-based indie band Arcade Fire and the various video and film streams related to it. With a track list that includes titles such as 'City with

No Children,' 'Empty Room', 'Rococo', 'Suburban War', 'Sprawl I (Flatland)' and, of course, 'The Suburbs', the CD reads more like the list of studio options in an architecture school than a typical sex, drugs and rock & roll LP. Win

Butler, the band's lead singer and songwriter, went so far as to say the 'album is neither a love letter to, nor an indictment of, the suburbs – it's a letter from the suburbs', sounding more like Rem Koolhaas than Rem Koolhaas himself.[2] The echo stems from the fact that Koolhaas strategically

Arcade Fire, still from
Scenes from the Suburbs, 2011

withholds both judgement and affect when discussing architectural structures often either denigrated or simply neglected by the discipline, from escalators to dumb boxes, precisely in order to showcase their fundamental role in the formation of the contemporary subject. Butler's remark helps make it clear that it is precisely through this apparent dispassion that Koolhaas underscores the primary importance of architecture in shaping contemporary affective life.

Arcade Fire's concerns not only parallel those of contemporary architecture but the band explicitly relies on architecture to structure its own thinking. This intellectual proximity is clearest in the CD's media appendages, where the drive towards keeping up becomes most interesting, revealed as a productive drive rather than merely a symptom. The band's webpage for *The Suburbs* has an image of a vintage car windshield framing a suburban landscape, and the moment a cursor touches it the still image jumps to flicker-book life, switching at a rapid pace from one view of the automotiveally mediated suburb to another.

Rather than drive towards suburbia, the car sits still, watching suburbia spin and speed out of control. This montage reverses our expectations of what does and does not move, of what is able to generate cultural speed and what remains a passive sitter-by. The CD's cover offers an analogue version of a similar role-reversal: released in eight variants allocated at random to purchasers of the album, the CD's dispersal used the regularity of the mail system to disseminate unexpected variation across suburbia.

Further underscoring that it is the suburbs – not media and their supporting technological matrix – that are speeding ahead, is the title track's video, directed by Spike Jonze. Made in Austin, Texas, and composed of selections from Jonze's short film *Scenes from the Suburbs*, the video depicts a revisionist history of the suburbs, a tale not of its rise and fall – the rise is totally edited out, with only the vintage car on the CD cover representing its heyday in 1950s America – but of the emergence (vaguely dated by other songs on the album to the 1970s) of an unanticipated suburban potential rushing into apocalypse. This aborted Eden is a landscape of such ennui that it produces tremendous, if compensatory, creative force. For the boys idling through the generic neighbourhood, every boring and repeated detail, from bike to kerb to cul de sac, is an opportunity for misuse and reappropriation, the very repetition creating skill rather than dullness. For example, the kerb cuts that typify the suburban streetscape – set in place to assure stability as a driver moves from the private and often elevated surface of a driveway to the public and lower domain of the street – become opportunities to perform aerial bike tricks, just as the ubiquitous porosity of chain link, which makes it unclear what is being kept out and what is being kept in, provides moments of surreal fantasy.

The video's initial lyrical mood, in a familiar trope, masks the encroaching proverbial hell – helicopters, flashlights and violence – that will quickly transform yesterday's suburbia into just about any place in today's headlines. But while the video's direct content replays a conventional narrative will known from *Poltergeist* to *The Truman Show* about the soporific effects of suburbia and the developer's use of visual norms to mask rapacious speculation: generic suburban housing is shown surrounded by ravaged empty land – the video's effect is to reveal the suburbs as having long since outlived such fictional distinctions. Utopia's bucolic past and an impending post-urban dystopia collapse to produce the ground for a new affect in the present that belongs to neither time zone.

Like Aesop's tale of the tortoise and the hare, the cloudburst of Arcade Fire's media-driven architectural theory reorders the race, and hence reshuffles the rapport between new media and old buildings. If typically buildings are slow and media fast, Chris Milk's interactive film *The Wilderness Downtown*, which functions as the music video for 'We Used to Wait', another track on Arcade Fire's suburban CD, radically disrupts these expected rates of speed. Using Google's Chrome browser as its interface, the film begins on an almost blank window framed in one corner by some branches and occasionally animated by flocks of birds. The address bar asks the user to enter the zip code of the home in which they grew up. Hit play, and new windows pop open at random intervals and in various locations and sizes across the monitor. The first is a tracking shot of a male jogger running at night on the black asphalt of a city street, slick with water. Subsequent windows show GPS footage of the zip code previously entered, both aerial and eye-level elevations drawn from Google Maps and Google Street View. The jogger on the ground, vision restricted by a hood and presumably the viewer's avatar, continues to run while the birds, presumably with the view of the satellites, continue to soar during this desynchronised trip down an updated memory lane. After a detour through a Deleuzian writing machine, which asks the user to write to his or her younger self, the film returns to the jogger who is now a boy running on a white ground. At this point, the entire proliferation of on-screen windows is slowly overgrown by virtual trees, which ultimately cover not only the boy's snowy world but his future city, producing the eponymous wilderness downtown.

The video relies on the sense of disjunction between the nostalgia that is presumed to be provoked by the images of the place you grew up (also presumed to be no longer the place you live) and the alienation presumed to be provoked by witnessing your past being interpolated into the super contemporary world of music video and GPS imaging technology.[3] Yet however much the film anticipates producing estrangement through these temporal displacements, reminiscent of an eighteenth-century drawing of an unbuilt building as ruin, the uncanny is by now too familiar a trope to yield that effect. Instead, a new feeling is generated by the cumulative effect of the different rates of cultural speed recorded by the various pop-up windows: the pace of technology, the flicker of representation, the drag of memory and the projective cast of desire. The effect is less like the cognitive dissonance of the uncanny or the frustration of envy, and more like a suburban symphony performed by a loose coalition of similar instruments playing at different tempos. From the shiny Chrome splash page – an interface where the processor-heavy film subverts the user's expectations of high speed and instant gratification – to the comments on the band's site – where viewers discuss Google Earth's inability to keep up with the rapid pace of architectural transformation in their hometowns – the film orchestrates the wide range of durations we all manage almost without note but that set the rhythms of life.

Today's increasingly fluid sense of time is transforming the contemporary from the last tick made by a clock into a continuously produced and shifting affect. Cultural expectations embedded in the suburban logic we occupy, no matter where we live, define media as the avant-garde, intrinsically ahead of our time, and sped up by technological motors, while architecture is assumed to lag behind, slowed down by mass, gravity and entropy. But these expectations rest on a fundamental category mistake: the avant-garde, a phenomenon predicated on fast and slow, ahead and behind, belongs to the fantasy of bohemia, an isolated milieu that according to Clement Greenberg made it possible for artists to 'assert themselves … aggressively … against the prevailing standards of society'.[4] The logic of the suburbs, by contrast, revolves around repetition and small variations that are often hard to measure. There is no inside or outside in the suburbs, no for or against, just a constant if irregular pulse. The architecture/media milieus seen through Arcade Fire suggests that in the suburban present, it is media that cannot keep up with the architects, who have long since understood that fleeting acts of perception undo all efforts to control speed or to judge which nose first crossed the finish line.

First published in *JSAH*, September 2011

NOTES

1. 'Keeping up with the Joneses' was created in 1916 by Arthur 'Pop' Mom for the *New York World* and ran in various American newspapers until 1944.

2. Cited in *NME Magazine* 52267 (31 July 2010), 24. Arcade Fire is known for its general media savvy. They were among the first to broadcast performances live via YouTube, commissioning digital visuals, or what they call Synchronised Artwork, to accompany the purchase of the album, developing blogs to support Haiti and other political causes.

3. The temptation to put in any address other than the one you grew up in, where you are now, where you might wish to be, is overwhelming.

4. Clement Greenberg, 'Avant-Garde and Kitsch', in *Art and Culture* (Boston, MA: Beacon Press, 1961), 5.

ARCHITECTURE BESIDE ITSELF (2012)

Contemporary painting is a subject requiring some courage to tackle, since we are said to have bid goodbye to painting as such many years ago. Yet art historian David Joselit has recently argued that the medium has reinvigorated its cultural potency by moving beyond, outside and beside itself.[1] On the one hand he theorises this movement as a literal expansion of the territory of painting, for example works that extend beyond a flat canvas to consider the various technical and structural apparatus required to support that substrate (walls, studs and pillars inside the walls, the paint on those walls, etc) as well as the position of the canvas in space. At the same time, Joselit argues that this movement exposes all the materialities that sit beside the limits of painting (as someone like Clement Greenberg defined them) to productively engage painting in the socio-economic, institutional and political forces that are more manifest and identifiable in this para-painterly territory. From this logic, clear criteria emerge for distinguishing between paintings that expand the medium in physical terms, such as by making the canvas three-dimensional, with the goal of reinforcing the autonomy of painting's specificity, and those that expand painting more conceptually, in order to engage its specific attributes with a broader cultural project. In other words, he makes clear how painting – when beside itself – can say goodbye and hello at the same time.

But whatever clarity this argument may offer contemporary painting, it suggests some conundrums for contemporary architecture. First, if painting is no longer itself, what is architecture, which has long since modelled itself on painting, to do? From Michael Graves and Juan Gris, to Zaha Hadid and Kazimir Malevich – or even Rem

Koolhaas and David Hockney, or Ben van Berkel and Francis Bacon – painting has served as the diagram for a broad spectrum of postwar architectural projects. Does the fact that painting is no longer painting invalidate this once productive cross-disciplinary emulation? Or, in contrast, does it suggest a way out of a frustrating paradox? Some have argued that when used as a model for architecture, the optical flatness of modernist painting (which is said to have advanced the project of painting) kept architecture within the compositional flatness of the Beaux-Arts drawing. Rather than advancing the architectural project, this flatness has been accused of encouraging architecture to prefer the controlling power of the plan rather than the participatory potential of space.[2] If architecture were finally to model itself on something more fulsome, the net result should theoretically be something more attentive to what is sometimes called 'lived experience.' Maybe the loss of painting as a viable model instead confirms the prescience of architects like Bernard Tschumi or Elizabeth Diller and Ric Scofidio, who heeded painting's adieux and modelled themselves on emergent mediums such as performance and new media art. Or at least they were better readers of art theory than, say, Rosalind Krauss's expanded field essay, in which painting was utterly irrelevant, not even appearing in the famous diagramming of the various things in relation to which architecture was defined. Finally, what if all these conflicting possibilities simply indicate that painting and everything it stands for – whether above, below or beside itself – is a non-issue for architecture? Perhaps today architecture has better things to do than bother with painting's anxiety about how to keep itself relevant.

It could indeed mean all those things, except for one fact: when painting moved beside itself it got a whole lot closer to architecture. To confront the complex isomorphisms between institutions and the built structures that give them actuality, to take responsibility for the ways in which objects in space cause fluctuations in the social environment, and to understand that the organisation of institutional space is never given or stable but rather emerges from the dynamic interaction between its characters and the events that take place within it, is, among other things, to assume an architectural posture. So, on the one hand, painting's move beside itself at least produces, if it does not a priori rely on, a definition of architecture and its agency. Such a definition could hardly be called irrelevant to architecture, if only in terms of revealing how architecture is perceived by others – a vantage point that is particularly telling when occupied by such an intimate interlocutor. This development also suggests that the vectors between architecture and painting have been reversed, making architecture more likely to serve as model for painting than the other way around. (If architecture were, in emulation of this new breed of painting, to occupy space, consider its structure in new terms, and add social performativity to its mix, architecture would become, well, architecture.) The change in polarity is significant because in contrast to convergences between architecture and sculpture (no less complex but rather common) intercourse between painting and architecture has not been especially potent since the architecture of perspective first offered itself as a structure for painting, however many parallels between the two recent generations of architects have sought to develop. Architecture now seems to offer something as a model that has not hitherto been considered valuable. Or at least architecture now exists within a less clearly established hierarchy of who's on first amongst the arts.

In order to ascertain what this potentially coveted architectural attribute might be, it is important to pause for a moment on the question of what it means to be beside yourself, whether the 'you' in question is painting, sculpture or anything else. If modernist definitions of medium relied on singular absolutes, while postmodernist definitions of what came to be called disciplines relied on the opposition between two terms, the thing beside itself depends on both. The idiom generally means to be so consumed by an emotion that normal rationality is lost. This displacement of generic subjectivity is more specifically defined by transactional analysis to describe the process whereby one part of the self observes another. This view assumes, in other words, that the self is not a unified structure but is made of various parts that can achieve some degree of autonomy, using this distance to witness each other in action. To be beside oneself, then, suggests an intensification of the affective state of the subject, a kind of singular absolute, as well as the exfoliation of the subject into diversified and multiple assemblages of selves – the self as defined in relation to other selves. Joselit emphasises the diversification of painting through its accretion of additional attributes – performance, institutional critique, etc – but these added capacities remain attendant to the painting they sit beside, reinforcing and transforming painting at the same time.

To manage such a dual action – promoting both its own specificity and its own transformation, therein discovering what it has that others may want – architecture has to confront what was once a liability: the fact that it has always been beside itself. This quality can now be exploited as an advantage. Initiating the still unfolding effort to distinguish building from manual labour and other forms of service and servitude, Vitruvius defined architecture as a combination of a wide variety of knowledge sets and practices, making the architect less a master of a single thing and more a manager of the many things that lie just outside and beside the name. By the Renaissance, architecture went even more beside itself as building and architecture came apart to constitute related but distinct entities. Architecture sat beside building, often literally sitting beside everyday structures, constituting itself as a special case, a more intense version of building as such. Architecture was never accused of having lost its wits, but the discipline was certainly considered to be building that operated according to an extra-quotidian form of reasoning. Simultaneously, the architect was increasingly associated with the production of texts and drawings about – and beside – the less and less primary built object. The developing versatility, not to say extreme diversification of architecture is well captured in this description of an opera by Bernini, where in addition to building the theatre 'he painted the scenes, cut the Statues, invented the Engines, composed the Musique, [and] writ the Comedy … all himselfe'.[3]

Since architecture has always been beside itself, its historic expertise in the extra-architectural has made it consistently open to opportunities beyond the limits of the field. This openness is particularly visible in architecture's substantial engagement with the range of new media that now compete with painting for its attention and that offer a massive and previously unavailable catalogue of procedures and effects. Film is primary among them. Just as architects were early adopters of paper, they have been making films ever since film was invented (filmmakers, too, have been casting architecture as protagonists since film antiquity), adding it to their always expanding range of doppelgangers, prostheses, substitutes, phantom limbs, costumes and avocations.[4] And because, in addition to their structural rapport with versatility, architects have historically also been attracted to novel gadgets, emerging technologies and as vast an array of media as money can buy, the convergence of film and architecture is in some respects the perfect storm of architectural desire. But the very historicity of this convergence means that it is not film in general that is driving architecture beside itself. Instead, certain capacities of film are being used by architects to overwhelm the field into motion, moving it over and allowing it to sit next to itself, existing in and operating on the world through a newly diffuse state of being. And these capacities relate not to film in itself, but to film in its own state of diffusion, film performing like other things, film not as autonomous medium but film, too, beside itself.

Contemporary architectural filmmaking generally falls into two categories, distinct in their relation both to architecture and to film. As films sit beside architecture, they sit on either side according to a logic that loosely resembles pre- and post-production work. In filmmaking this sequence is defined as preparatory planning, the recording of raw footage and the subsequent collapsing of sound and the like into an integrated form. In other words, it describes a working process in which each phase may vary in duration but must conclude in a final film. The distribution, screening and viewing of the film itself are post-post-production, so to speak, but the chronological stability of the sequence secures the status of the resultant film as conclusive, tellingly referred to in Hollywood parlance as 'locked'. In architecture, at least during the first era of its filmic dalliance, the pre-production phase too was first and belonged to the design process and the post-production phase took place after the period of construction. Thus, early Bauhaus films belong to the logic of pre-production, revealing in the case of Moholy-Nagy's *Light-Space Modulator,* for example, a series of experiments that describe potentials to be actualised elsewhere. Later films, from Moholy-Nagy's own *New Architecture of the London Zoo* to Pierre Chenal and Le Corbusier's *Architecture d'Aujourd'hui* and even Charles Eames' *House: After Five Years of Living,* operate according to the logic of architectural post-production, giving instructions on the proper mode of inhabitation for modern buildings themselves conceived in filmic terms.[5] While in most of these cases the architect cannot quite bring himself to leave the scene entirely and give the building over fully to an audience, both pre- and post-production take their place in the architectural chain of being in relation to the built object and its autonomy.

During the period of the neo-avant-garde – when architectural filmmaking became a technique widely used by radical groups, along with pneumatics, performance and pop-up cities – the logic of pre- and post-production was tendentiously collapsed into a notion of meta (if not mega) product. The purpose of this shift was to dispense with the object entirely. Storyboards replaced drawings, scenario planning became design, and a projected environment became the final event. If early modernist films emphasised the autonomy of form and the radical independence of space by absorbing the outside world and drawing it within architecture, neo-avant-garde films did the reverse. The films of Superstudio, Haus Rucker, and others, or even the film stills later deployed by Bernard Tschumi, all acted to depict the dissolution of architecture into a class of non-objects, producing film instead of architecture, film without architecture.

Aspects of the logic of pre- and post-production still obtain today yet, taking place in the context of an increasingly variable notion of the architectural event, their effect is to destabilise rather than clarify the centrality of built work or objecthood. Some architects produce post-produced films, with sound and lighting effects, at even very preliminary stages of design. In fact, films with sound tracks, rapidly changing weather and other dramatic lighting effects are often required by competitions. Other architects specify animated projections as permanent components of their designs as if specifying glass, steel or any other material (just as some filmmakers specify the architecture that will house their projections as if buildings were one type of screen among many). And of course, hyperrealist animated renderings often completely obliterate *an observer's* capacity to determine whether the thing being filmed is a building, a physical model or a virtual wish. Taken as a set, pre- and post-production films fail to confirm the finality of the construction of a building or verify the cohesiveness of a scheme, nor do they anticipate a final product or describe a stable sequence. Rather they sit beside architecture, or even surround it, simultaneously making it more visible and diffusing its reception.

If architectural filmmaking today occupies variable positions in the temporal unfolding of the architectural event, thereby rendering the architectural object multiplicitous and unstable, these architectural films also relate to film's traditions and history. Contemporary pre-production work derives most immediately not from a filmic archive as such, but rather from the animations produced in the early days of digital design. The initial development of companies such as Softimage, which in 1988 issued the first platform that enabled modelling, animation and rendering to take place in a single integrated environment, allowed architects to 'film' processes such

MOS, *Element House*, prototype, 2010

as particles exploding across the screen, branching systems running rhizomatically rampant, and crowds swarming into formation. The images were often deliberately unrendered, left in a state of exaggerated visual primitivism and utterly lacking in post-production to suggest that the forms were wholly unmediated. These animations, in other words, were staged such that they would be received as aligned with information and its visualisation, as if operating within a scientist rather than representational paradigm. The architect ceased to imagine him or herself as a designer or even as a director. Instead he or she was a writer of code, the instigator of a happening without a script and most importantly a spectator, observing at a distance the drama of data and its shaping. The architect became a witness to architecture, using film to carve out a new role and to produce a new territory beside itself.

But however much the apparent artlessness of these animations was presented as due to the supposedly unaestheticised domain of computer software codes and processes, however much this type of film is intended to make architecture appear, if not deus-ex machina, then materia-ex machina, these animations also evolved out of the modernist identification of art with science, an identification in which film played an important role. Siegfried Ebeling, for example, who was a student at the Bauhaus in the 1920s, argued for a then unusual biological and ecological basis for design, defining the house as 'the medium of passage for a continual flow of … energies', just as filmmakers from Walter Ruttmann to Viking Eggeling were patenting animation devices and making films that animated abstract shapes and patterns as if by a continual flow of internal energy.[6] Rather than an artefactual result of contemporary parametric design, the animation of figures that operate according to some notion of natural law is a return to film's history and the history of film's relation to architecture.

And of course it is this proximity and repetition that makes evident the radical difference between those few early animations and the virtually infinite quantity of digital animation produced today. While they share an identification with scientific discourses and a reduced visual palette – often blank backgrounds with little attention paid to depth of field, no environmental accoutrement, few details and less surface texture – the early films never trace a change to or in form but rather only its constant self-balancing. Focusing on elements of visual composition, pure shapes against the abstraction of empty space, geometry has nothing in these films but itself to contend with. They convert immanent critique of cells, lines and membranes into immanent choreography as they maintain the self-containedness of their subject and serve as the basis for an architecture of absolute autonomy: they are films of architecture within itself.

Despite the anatomical isomorphism between contemporary animations and these modernist symphonies of abstraction, today's productions are distinct in always diagramming the mutually constitutive feedback between form and external forces. The new films describe the evolution of a particular form produced within an active environment rather than the movement of stable and generic forms in evacuated space. They hence have an intrinsically narrative – though not necessarily linear or predictable – structure in which something (often catastrophic) happens that causes things to change their course. Gravity, collapse, exploding population densities, air currents, movements of money and flows of social desire all perform on film, demonstrating their agency for the architectural camera. These animations are thus subject to the index of time, to the march of entropy; they show architecture as forces beyond its control overcome it and so produce architecture beside itself.

Pre-production films, then, have a peculiar double ontology with respect to architecture: first, they stand beside rather than before the architectural event, destabilising its temporal location and priority. Second, they transform the architect into a witness and an observer (however naïve or canny) of complex and unpredictable phenomena. Moreover, these animations have a highly sophisticated visual repertoire of the archaic and artless, as though they were engineered sketches, pre-produced objects like Beaux-Arts *esquisses* on their way to being post-produced into something else. Yet every step of the Beaux-Arts process was structured to produce the myth of architectural mastery – over history, over material, over composition. The simplicity of the original sketch intentionally contrasted with the polished sophistication of the final product. The contemporary filmic *esquisse*, on the other hand, reveals multiplicity and subjection both in the nature of the architectural object and its producer.

If pre-production films tend towards the archaic and the animated, post-production films tend toward the supercinematic and an almost hysterical hyperrealism. Increasingly naturalistic lighting effects, convincing texture mapping, and fewer and fewer of the once ubiquitous impossible fly-through camera angles produce a new suspension of disbelief: the spectator is invited to lose judgement about whether the object appearing before him or her is real. While necessarily part of the architect's bag of tricks, and highly effective in persuading clients that a project should be built, the collapse of the real and the virtual is not only a marketing device. More and more, as the digital processes that produce these films overlap with the digital processes that produce the building elements of construction, the real and the virtual are losing their distinct status. By generating an inability to distinguish between a model and a building, the films not only reiterate the increasingly problematic nature of the architectural event but also provoke a kind of crisis of spectatorship, calling for new forms of attention and observation. Common features of these films, such as their extremely slow camera pan, extra-wide aspects and ultra-high resolution, produce not information but rather detail overload. If Walter Benjamin claimed for architecture a distracted form of attention, these films claim so much attention that any sense of focus or hierarchy is overwhelmed. Architecture in this supersaturated visual field is like building and its representation, sandwiched side by side, architecture and itself.

This pressure on architecture is all the more acute today, when filmmaking by architects is becoming an everyday means of visual communication. The architectural film has supplanted the drawing, has become the drawing, and has in some practices displaced the whole repertoire of traditional architectural forms of representation. Sketches and analytical diagrams, construction documents and models, site analysis and final presentation: all are now made almost exclusively and virtually incidentally of moving images. This everydayness may indicate the triumph of media and spectacle over all else, but it has certainly enticed many professional practitioners to forget their representational Ps & Qs and fall victim to a technologically reinvigorated positivism.

On the other hand, for some architects today, the ubiquity of architectural filmmaking is a means of developing representational ruses that slip right next to conventional professional protocols and by their discrete adjacency recalibrate the way architecture exists in and operates on the world. The New York-based MOS, for example, a studio garnering increasing attention for its wide variety of architectural films, goes far to exploit the fact that architecture now exists beside itself. Today architecture as object, architect as producer and the public/ user/consumer/viewer of architecture have together and – all at once – become an array of selves that stand side by side one another as witnesses, testifying to the particular form of instrumentality of each and at least occasionally becoming ecstatic at their potentially combined agencies. Every one of these moments of 'besidedness' disrupts not only the routine operations of the field, but the routinisation of life as such, towards which so much of architecture's standard professional practice contributes. Indeed, one of the most important effects of architecture as it goes beside itself is the way in which this movement multiplies how the architectural subject is constituted.

It is an indication of their interest in this question that one of the primary features distinguishing MOS's films from the general context in which they belong is the addition of elements driven by character and personality, if not passion: talk show formats, strange romances gone awry, deadpan humour and the withholding of the human voice in favour of subtitles all toy with varying notions of subjectivity. And it is in this constitution of the subject that the relationship not only of architecture to film, but of both to painting returns as a question.

Film is typically identified with an almost universal audience. Many architects have what might be called film envy, which is generally related less to film and its making than to its reception: popular, portable and profitable beyond any architectural expectation. Painting has historically been assured an audience by its cultural status and gravitas, but the scope of its reception has rarely competed with that of films. But painting, unlike film, which is understandably satiated by its success, increasingly desires users, fearful of losing its agency in a world increasingly full of images (and moving images at that).

This desire for users and the utility they purport to confer is what entices painting to assume an architectural posture. Ironically, architecture, before it had clients – even before it was architecture, as we understand it today – had lots of users, nothing but users. Yet it wanted an audience, a viewer, even a single spectator. These different forms of desire may ultimately have less to do with mediums and formats than with how the instrumental capacity of culture is defined. But in a world increasingly anxious about utility the capacity to configure audiences, users and spectators simultaneously – a capacity honed by the particularities of architecture's genealogy and magnified by its current filmic additions – is being seen as more and more, well, useful.

FLASH IN THE PAN

Reyner Banham, an early advocate for film-making in architecture, argued that the only way for architecture to keep up with the accelerated cultural speeds of the postwar world was to get out of what he referred to, tellingly, as the black box of professional practice and give itself over to an architecture *autre*.[7] Today we can say instead that by simultaneously and variously engaging the internal logic of the box, the box itself, and its output, architecture is no longer a field focusing on routes by which to escape itself; rather it is exploring the many possibilities of becoming an architecture *à côté*.

First published in Michael Meredith and Hilary Sample (eds), *Everything All at Once: The Software, Videos and Architecture of MOS* (New York: Princeton Architectural Press, 2013)

NOTES

1. David Joselit, 'Painting Beside Itself', *October* 130 (Fall 2009), 125–34.

2. This is a theme explored by Yves-Alain Bois in various contexts, but perhaps most forcefully in his 'A Picturesque Stroll around Clara-Clara' in *October* 29 (Summer 1984), 32–62.

3. Described by John Evelyn following his trop to Rome in 1644 and cited in DA Beecher, 'Gianlorenzo Bernini's "The Impresario": The Artist as the Supreme Trickster', in the *University of Toronto Quarterly* 53 (1984), 236–47.

4. There is a growing yet not fully systematic literature on the history of film in architecture. Some titles include François Penz & Maureen Thomas, *Cinema & Architecture* (London: British Film Institute, 1997), Maggie Toy (ed), *AD 64: Architecture and Film* (1994); Bob Fear (ed), *AD 70: Architecture + Film II* (2000); Katherine Shonfield, *Walls Have Feelings: Architecture, Film and the City* (London: Routledge, 2000) and Dietrich Neumann et al, *Film Architecture* (Munich: Prestel, 1996).

5. Beatriz Colomina has written essential accounts of both Le Corbusier and Eames in relation to these films. See her *Privacy and Publicity: Modern Architecture as Mass Media* (Cambridge, MA: MIT Press, 1996) and 'Enclosed by Images' in *Grey Room* 2 (Winter 2001), 6–29.

6. On the broad subject of science and representation, see Bruce Clark and Linda Henderson (eds), *From Energy to Information: Representation in Science and*

Technology, Art and Literature (Stanford CA: Stanford University Press, 2001) and Luc Pauwels, *Visual Culture of Science: Rethinking Representational Practices* (Hanover, NH: Dartmouth College Press, 2005). Siegfried Ebeling's 1926 text *Space as Membrane* was published by Architectural Association Publications in 2010. See more particularly, Christoph Asendorf, 'Bodies in Force Fields: Design Between the Wars', in Bruce Clarke and Linda Dalrymple Henderson (eds), *From Energy to Information: Representation in Science and Technology, Art, and Literature* (Stanford, CA: Stanford University Press, 2002), 203. Finally, on film and architectural animation, see Greg Lynn, *Animate Form* (New York, NY: Princeton Architectural Press, 1999) and *Folds, Bodies and Blobs: Collected Essays* (Brussels: La Lettre volée, 1998).

7. Banham was generally known for his engagement with contemporary media and technology in architectural design and made a film himself, *Reyner Banham Loves Los Angeles*, London, BBC Documentary, 1972. On his use of the technological metaphor of the black box in his discussion of the overdetermined biases of architectural practice, see his 'The Black Box: The Secret Profession of Architecture' in Mary Banham (ed), *A Critic Writes: Essays by Reyner Banham* (Berkeley, CA: University of California Press, 1996), 292–300. Finally, see also Nigel Whitely, 'Banham and Otherness: Reyner Banham and His Quest for an Architecture Autre', *Architectural History* 33 (1990), 188–221.

ARCHITECTURE *IN EXTREMIS* (2011)

In 1947 Langley Collyer was found dead in his home, rotting under 130 tons of 'stuff', having gotten caught in one of his own traps (set to keep out potential robbers, who might assume that a house almost filled solid with miscellaneous things must contain some treasures) while trying to bring some food to his paralysed brother Homer. By the time Langley was found, Homer had died too, of starvation. The Collyer brothers, who have a park in Harlem named after them as well as a firefighter's term (houses crowded with dangerously flammable quantities of things are called 'Collyer's mansions'), are the most famous early case study in what is now called 'hoarding'. The term describes an increasingly public mania for collecting; to wit the slew of reality TV shows such as *Hoarders*, *Hoarding: Buried Alive* and even *Animal Hoarding*.[1] If every age has its favourite neurosis – from the agoraphobia and hysteria that took over the streets and homes of women at the turn of the last century to the multiple personality disorder that became the self-diagnosis of choice for the myriad readers or viewers of the 1970s, again mostly women, who encountered *Sibyl* in book or movie form – hoarding is the turn of this century's craze *du jour* afflicting everyone from Imelda Marcos to Angelina Jolie (how many children does it take to go from having a family, to a collection, to a problem?)

If every age has its symptomatic symptom, every age also has its symptomatic cure. Today, as one pop culture website put it, 'clean up crews are the new rehab'.[2] The pageantry of cleaning house is now therapeutic entertainment. Of course, domestic hygiene has always been a subject promoted, regimented and enforced by architecture and interior design. But now it is spectacularised, acquiring a new exhibition value that requires strategies of display, like reality TV, as well as medicalised, a status that requires official diagnostic classification rather than the kind of 'how to deal with your clutter' advice offered by Martha Stewart. Indeed, the tidy-up tradition of interior decorating manuals that runs from Elsie de Wolf to *Dwell* magazine has taken a radical turn. Bad interiors are now considered to be not just in bad taste but actually bad for your health. In 2013, hoarding entered the revised fifth edition of the *Diagnostic and Statistical Manual of Mental Disorders* (for an ailment, the equivalent of 'making it' onto the walk of nutty fame). This inclusion transformed hoarding into a recognised medical condition rather than just an odd way of being in the world, an extreme way of designing your living space (hoarding typically although not exclusively takes place at home), or the gambit of every successful museum director. Hoarding's newfound legitimacy is itself a symptom of a profound shift in the study of psychology. The handful of case studies Freud once worked from has become an almost infinite and expanding number of categories of symptoms and maladies: in the 1840s there were two types of mental disorder according to the US census, idiocy and insanity, but by the 1990s there were almost 300 categories in the *DSM*, which required almost one thousand pages for their classification, competing with *S,M,L,XL* for biggest book on the shelf status. Maybe the psychiatric profession has a hoarding problem and the *DSM* is its *wunderkammer*.

Over the years certain kinds of neurotics have been more attracted to architecture than others, just as some neuroses have in turn attracted more architectural attention than others. This mirroring rapport not only reflects, but has helped produce the historically evolving ways in which the limit conditions of architecture have been defined. For example, just as agoraphobia and early modern theories of urbanism produced mutually reinforcing notions of the proper use and organisation of space in the burgeoning metropolis, the theory that decoration was a displacement of erotic impulses (and hence should be banned from architectural expression) gained currency during the same era and as architecture was increasingly understood as an autonomous discipline. These reciprocities assisted in the definition of architecture as a medium constructed out of a limited number of constituent elements mirrored in and reinforced by subjects defined by a psyche composed of a prescribed number of behaviours and feelings.[3] Similarly, the panopticon, which establishes architecture not as a medium but as a virtual system of discipline orchestrating the construction of social relations, is itself a diagram of the spatial relationships between inmates as well as of their relationship to architecture, gazing at, even internalising, the shifting borders of its expanded field. More recently this kind of projective identification between self and structure enabled a convergence between sustainability and so-called 'sick building syndrome' – wherein occupants fall ill but buildings are called sick – which produced and was produced by an emerging theory of architecture as environment that turns space into habitat and users into just one register of a continuous biota ranging in scale and species from genetic building blocks to the building conceived as organism.

Hoarding, however, while showing perhaps even more obvious overlaps with architectural concerns, has been less successful in finding its architectural mate. This despite the fact that hoarders collect at home, their activities necessarily taking place within an architectural frame. Hoarding is a direct challenge to the regimes of structural stability (buildings collapse or go up in flames when overstuffed), the free plan (open space becomes only an invitation to hoard) and hygiene (one man's collection is another man's garbage) embedded in modern architecture. Modern buildings can almost be described as an assemblage of elements, from built-ins to garages, that are prophylactics shielding architecture against any impending sign of a propensity to hoard.

The history of architecture is full of famous examples of the union between architecture and hoarding. These include innumerable cabinets of curiosities stuffed full and then stuffed into buildings, as well as the strange fact that 'cabinet' itself used to mean room when such chambers were subjects of wonder and curiosity, but was downgraded to a boring piece of furniture when an increasingly stuff-averse architecture began dealing in space rather than rooms and a rationalist mentality evacuated wonder not merely from architecture but from the world itself. Despite this overwhelming drive to clean house, the history of architecture is full of figures who used significant quantities of objects to produce architectural effects and sometimes even effects of wonder: from Sir John Soane's excessive collection of antique fragments, books, mirrors and buildings – his house was a collection of houses, filled with a collection of collections – to Andy Warhol,

Verner Panton's
Pantotower, c1968

who organised his possessions architecturally – superstars and paintings at the sparkly Silver Factory, cookie jars and god-knows-what-else at the red plush home – to Ray Eames and her almost infinite number of toys, carpets, dolls and pictures, which she was constantly rearranging – to Verner Panton, who, when photographed in his wildly psychedelic interiors, seems in danger of sharing the fate of Langley Collyer, ending up crushed by his piles of shaggy, shelly, serpentine stuff.

The exclusion of this history of hoarding from standard accounts of the development of contemporary architecture reflects the fact that hoarding is not just a matter of collecting, or even excessive collecting. Hoarding exposes the architectural effects of excess and shows how they constitute a specific modality of production. A key feature of these effects, one that distinguishes hoarding from other forms of approximate architecture, is that they derive neither from media nor from the building envelope or surface but rather from things. Even though 'things' do not at first appear to be architectural because they do not contribute directly to either the construction or the

205

inhabitation of buildings, they set effects in motion that activate relations between bodies and objects in space, structure the perception of space, and alter patterns of circulation and use. It is precisely the potential of things to encroach on these capabilities, which architecture generally considers its domain, that both accounts for this exclusion and produces the opportunity to convert hoarding into a theory of architecture.

Whether or not its effects begin with an architectural intention or from a case of disposophobia, the compulsive inability to get rid of things, hoarding produces architecture that does not consider function to be a generative principle, nor does it find pleasure in playing with programme and meaning – two foundational concepts of architecture, at least since modernism. Hoarding instead focuses attention away from use and representation and towards the materiality of things, subjecting them to a form of design that has its own techniques and logics.

The most important things about hoarding in this context are, first, that it is rooted in objecthood. The approach to the object's status in art, which is tied to questions about its relationship to space both real and illusory, has changed radically since emerging as an articulated problem in art theory during the 1960s. This history, however, is rendered even more convoluted when considered in light of postwar architectural theory.[4] While architects, too, have struggled between approaching the object from a conceptual or a material standpoint, their conflict is compounded by the inevitable doubling of this dichotomy in the relationship between the products of architects (models, drawings and the like, today often the only part of the building process in direct contact with the architect, though even this contact is increasingly made through immaterial means and hence is both real and illusory) and the production of building (always physical and real but only loosely tied to the architect).[5] However much a meaty drawing of corrugated concrete by Paul Rudolph is concerned with the objecthood of its subject, it is inevitably immaterial compared to the building. The reverse is also true. While John Hejduk's Bye House might best be understood as a conceptual project divorced from material or matters of execution, the building inevitably lurked nearby, perhaps nearer than Hejduk could ever have imagined. The fact that even when executing a theoretical project Hejduk was inescapably also providing the proverbial blueprint for a physical structure was demonstrated by the almost grotesque posthumous construction of his design.

This kind of back and forth (back to a modernist definition of medium, forth to a post-structuralist definition of discipline) is now essential to architecture's current cultural status and thus to its post-medium specificity. Yet one of the most fundamental lessons of hoarding – the fact that upon inhabitation the building, as object, is instantly confronted and often impinged upon by a mass of other objects totally foreign to both building and architecture – has not been addressed. Such things are forcefully excluded from architectural consideration because the field has no way to admit that these objects have material lives that are not secondary additions to architecture, or merely instruments of personalisation or functional fulfilment: they are what gives rise to architecture in the first place. The interior is produced not by walls or other boundaries but by the order, array and number of objects within. It coalesces into a perceptible environment not despite their generally varied and unpredictable presence but by virtue of their objecthood, which remains resolutely independent from the envelope that contains them. While managing the 'emplacement' of upholstery, furnishings and interior surfaces was once part of the architect's repertoire, this was precisely the kind of curatorial knowledge eliminated from the field as it marched its way towards medium-specificity first and then disciplinarity (and hence virtuality) second. Hoarding, in other words, is not only an object-based practice but frames a new understanding of architecture's objecthood.

During what can now be called the medium-specific phase of modernism, architecture understood itself increasingly as a building-object, and decreasingly as a container for other objects. As architecture after this phase of modernism moved toward a post-medium condition, it flirted with dematerialisation in an effort to abandon its base link to object status altogether. One might even go so far as to say that architecture has fed its mania for becoming a dematerialised object by displacing the confrontation with the stubborn nature of things into fields to which it feels superior, like interior design, and relegating objects to the generally abject category of stuff. Hoarding subverts these various positions because it insists on a particularly obdurate kind of objecthood, one that is not (traditionally) architectural in scale or material but that nevertheless plays a primary role in the construction of the space around it – the space objects produce rather than are contained by. The composition of space, the movement of bodies within it, the character of the interior's visual field and the 'proper' or efficient unfolding of programme (all still deeply held architectural values) are largely determined by the things inside architecture. Even Sigfried Giedion, who arguably did more than anyone to usher in the era of architecture as a specific medium, alternately (and perhaps paradoxically) called 'stuff' both a constituent element of architecture and a transitory one. And indeed, stuff's deployment gives solidity as well as provisionality to architecture's nature as an object.[6]

Hoarding not only instigates a long overdue reconsideration of architecture and objecthood, but also offers a means of understanding the structure of today's visual field. On the one hand hoarding is a visual affront, eliciting horror, and reducing the viewer to a reluctant witness of the grotesque. On the other hand, and unlike the grotesque, hoarding does not register as an aesthetic event or as a phenomenon that requires any form of attention, even if only distracted attention. Hoarding, in fact, exceeds the implicit standards used to convert the everyday and its various and sundry acts of perception into an apperceptible visual encounter. While many things might be said to be hard to see in cultural terms, hoarding productively frames this challenge, because hoarding, unlike other forms of abjection, is explicitly defined in visual terms. Or rather, hoarding requires a visual diagnostic because the *DSM* relies on an unstated visual aesthetic regime to recognise the act.

The great expansion of the *DSM* in the 1970s relied on the inadvertent conversion of minimalist aesthetics into a psychiatric principle. Things become 'clutter' when they are displayed or archived in a way that does not adhere to the *DSM*'s visual standards. The inability to recognise this transgression of propriety in the visual field is the defining characteristic of the diagnosed hoarder. It is referred to as 'clutter blindness,' clutter having literally replaced hysteria in Freud's theory of conversion disorders. If the writers of the *DSM* had read a bit more widely in the history of art, they might have known that *horror vacui* was a perfectly respectable aesthetic mania, or rather principle, which led not to 'clutter' but to a fulsome and heterogeneous aesthetic atmosphere and system of display. Rococo surfaces of all sorts, eighteenth-century painting salons with pictures apparently placed slap-dash along their walls, and art nouveau interiors: all filled every possible square inch with often competing and disparate visual elements until they induced not clutter blindness but a kind of clutter euphoria. The need for restraint is of relatively recent vintage, yet is by now a holdover from an increasingly outmoded commitment to the aesthetic doctrine of 'what you see is what you get'. Hoarding, then, to anyone other than a minimalist, promises a means of design that might once again accommodate a plenum in the visual and spatial field.

A third theorem to be extracted from hoarding derives from the fact that hoarding does not use programme or function as a way to legislate the interaction between architecture and its occupants. Hoarders are defined as people who not only collect large quantities of objects – often the same kind of objects – but place them in 'inappropriate' places. A hoarder might have 50 frying pans, a reasonable number for a cook and to keep in a restaurant kitchen, but apparently a sign of neurosis if stored in a living room. And according to the *DSM*, hoarders not only put things in the programmatically wrong place but do so in such a way as to interrupt the flow of bodies in space. Their archives take up space normally intended for circulation and inhabitation in ways that often convert these voids into solid blocks, in a kind of Rachel Whiteread in reverse. Accordingly, hoarding might just as well be described as a critical resistance to the regimes of propriety typically enforced by architecture, or as a means of understanding space that does not just resist standard measures of use, but ignores them altogether. Through the process of densification, hoarding frees the interior from typical conventions of use – perhaps more radically than any deconstructionist analysis of 'dwelling', or at least with less ironic conviction – and permits the interior as such to drive architecture forward.

Finally, hoarding adheres not only to a logic of display, but specifically to a theory of animation. In addition to issues of quantity (how much is too much?), placement (as the *DSM* makes clear, clutter is just something in the wrong place) and value (collecting things that have no apparent value to others, which ironically is the dream of every art collector longing to buy cheap and sell high) hoarding describes an active relationship between collecting and exhibiting. Hoarders frequently move their things, locating objects not in a fixed position in relation to static architectural surroundings, but through a fluid network of relationships to other objects, themselves also shifting: this belongs here, on top of that pile, in the middle of this room. Most importantly, hoarders do what is called 'churning', taking things from the bottom of piles and placing them on top. The collections of hoarders, then, are in a constant state of rotation, not unlike the rotation of works of art from storage to gallery in contemporary museums. This animation, from an architectural point of view, gives the space of a hoarder a temporal flow that an architectural interior otherwise does not have. After all, churning amounts to a recognition that objects do not merely function to produce architectural ambiences but operate to keep them fluid; it offers building a measure of durational variation that the typical definitions of architecture lack. Hoarding, in other words, gives to architecture a field of specifically animated effects.

With all due respect to hoarding's victims it should be said that no one died from architecture lacking an adequately updated theory of medium-specificity. (Although it could also be said that Richard Neutra believed that what he called overly 'vigorous' interior design killed Emile Zola: too much stuff in the room, not enough air through the window.)[7] And yet architecture today cannot avoid entanglement with many urgent questions, some generated by external social forces and others from its own immanent critique. Contemporary architecture has long since ceased to be guided by strict and sure principle, which could reduce formal composition to a handful of rules, or organise an entire design approach around a single material or something else equally concrete and finite. This general tendency towards expansiveness of the last 50 years is changing direction and distancing architecture from its more recent past. The impulse to open architecture to new ideas, technologies and prospects that was dominant 20 years ago has now become a policy of *laissez-faire* indiscriminateness, resulting in pressing, if often undirected, attempts to define some new parameters for the field. So while we may not live or die under the weight of architectural ideas that, like a hoarder's pile of stuff, might be better placed in the trash, we do need to rearrange this immediate past and churn it into an active and productive archive. From within the narrow confines of either medium or discipline, it can be all too easy to forget that architecture has the capacity to be both something specific and something else at the same time, a dense nexus of materials, their systems of production and their consequences, as well as an attenuated network of ideas, actions and objects only loosely held together by the name. Imagining new definitions for architecture that include a bigger category of objects, a broader understanding of work and an expanded engagement with systems of instability and participation in the processes of design will not weaken architecture's cultural project but rather could make it more extreme.

First published in *Log* 22 (2011)

NOTES

1. For an overview of contemporary clinical psychiatric understandings of hoarding, see G Steketee and R Frost, 'Compulsive Hoarding: Current Status of Research', *Clinical Psychology Review* 23:7 (December 2003), 905–27.

2. Amelie Gillette, 'Hoarding Is So Hot Right Now,' www.avclub.com/articles/hoarding-is-so-hot-right-now-37868, accessed 11 January 2010.

3. In this essay, I use 'medium' to refer to the discourses around medium-specificity as defined and promoted by Clement Greenberg and 'discipline' to refer to later structural and post-structuralist definitions. I will leave the nomination of the current state of the field to the collective efforts of this volume. These questions have generated a significant literature, particularly in art history and media theory, a full listing of which is beyond the scope of this essay but which may be said to run the gamut from Gottfried Lessing's *Laocoon: An Essay on the Limits of Painting and Poetry* (Boston, MA: Roberts Brothers, 1877); to Rosalind Krauss, 'Reinventing the Medium,' *Critical Inquiry* 25:2 (Winter 1999), 289–305; and Nicolas Bourriaud's *Relational Aesthetics* (Paris: Presses du réel, 2002). *Kissing Architecture* (New York, NY: Princeton University Press, 2011) contains additional references.

4. The classic formulation is Michael Fried's 'Art and Objecthood', 1967, in Charles Harrison and Paul Wood (eds), *Art in Theory 1900–1990: An Anthology of Changing Ideas* (Cambridge, MA: Blackwell, 1992), 822–34.

5. This is the subject of much of Peter Eisenman's writings, which have been anthologised in *Eisenman Inside Out: Selected Writings, 1963–1988* (New Haven, CT: Yale University Press, 2004).

6. The difference between constituent and transitory architectural facts is worked through by Sigfried Giedion in 'The Present State in Architecture' and 'The New Space Conception' in *Space Time and Architecture: The Growth of a new Tradition* (Cambridge, MA: Harvard University Press, 1991), xliv–lvi.

7. See Lavin, *Form Follows Libido* (Cambridge, MA: MIT Press, 2004), 95.

INDEX

ACKNOWLEDGEMENTS

Few things are more subject to historical revision than descriptions of the present, and this collection of essays written over the course of more than a decade traces the vicissitudes of my engagement with this Sisyphean task. Because this effort entailed many of the different platforms through which my work unfolds, from teaching to scholarly research and criticism, there is an equally wide array of support I'd like to acknowledge. Many of these essays have been previously published or presented as lectures and I'd like to thank the numerous hosts who made room for this material. Students at UCLA, Princeton and the GSD were productive interlocutors at key moments in my thinking over the past 10 years. The Getty Research Institute and the Graham Foundation provided essential support for research. The editorial precision of Cynthia Davidson, Sarah Whiting, Julian Rose and Thomas Weaver brought lucidity where there was none and Sarah Hearne managed to conjure many of the images presented here apparently out of thin air. My intellectual friends and colleagues know who they are and that there are no words sufficient to express my thanks to them. Any nuggets of novelty that remain herein after this decade of sifting through the new are due to their support.

IMAGE SECTION

Claes Oldenburg, Bedroom Ensemble 2/3, 1963–69
Photo: Rudolf Nagel © 1963–69 Claes Oldenburg,
courtesy Museum für Moderne Kunst Frankfurt am Main,
former collection of Karl Ströher, Darmstadt (see p 34)

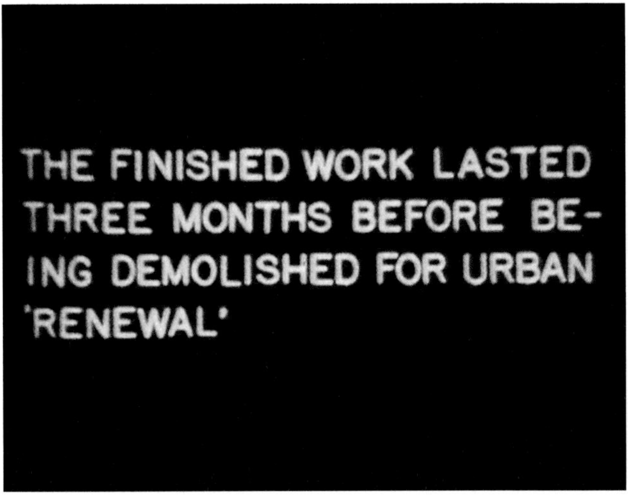

THE FINISHED WORK LASTED
THREE MONTHS BEFORE BE-
ING DEMOLISHED FOR URBAN
'RENEWAL'

Gordon Matta-Clark, *Splitting*, 1974 © 2014
Estate of Gordon Matta-Clark / Artists Rights Society (ARS), New York
Courtesy Electronic Arts Intermix (EAI), New York (see p 52)

André Bruyère and Fernand Léger, Perspective for a villa with three workshops, Village Polychrome, near Biot, France 1953, Canadian Centre for Architecture, gift in memory of Daniel Robbins © ADAGP, Paris and DACS, London 2014 (see p 63)

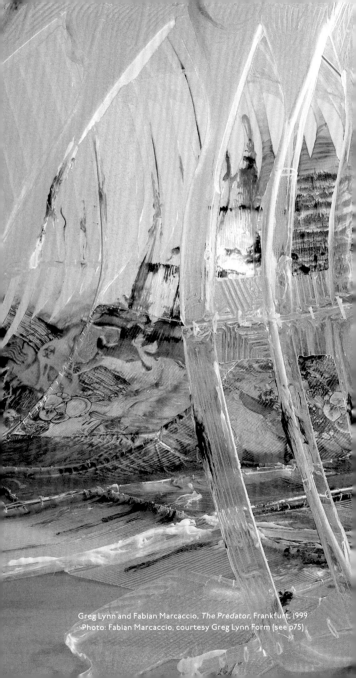

Greg Lynn and Fabian Marcaccio, *The Predator*, Frankfurt, 1999
Photo: Fabian Marcaccio, courtesy Greg Lynn Form (see p75)

Achille and Pier Giacomo Castiglioni, *Colori e Forme*
Nella Casa d'Oggi in Villa Olmo, Como, 1957
Courtesy Fondazione Achille Castiglioni (see p 86)

Achille and Pier Giacomo Castiglioni, RAI at the Milan Fair, 1965
Courtesy Fondazione Achille Castiglioni (see p 89)

Achille and Pier Giacomo Castiglioni, RAI Pavilion at the Milan Fair, 1966
Courtesy Fondazione Achille Castiglioni (see p 89)

N ANNO CIO' CHE UN TEMPO
I RIUSCIVA A VEDERE
EL CORSO DI UNA VITA
E ALLA

Achille and Pier Giacomo Castiglioni, RAI Pavilion at the Milan Fair, 1968
Courtesy Fondazione Achille Castiglioni (see p 90)

Achille Castiglioni, Casa del Fascio, 1939–40
Courtesy Fondazione Achille Castiglioni (see p 93)

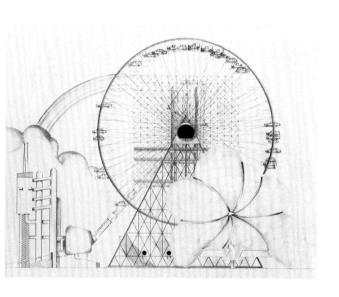

Alessandro Poli, side elevation of the Piper, c1966, Alessandro Poli fonds,
Canadian Centre for Architecture © CCA (see p 99)

Caveada, Fiumi, Galli and Lorenzi, work produced in Leonardo Savioli's Interior
Architecture (Architettura degli Interni) course in 1966/67. That year's theme
was Il Pipe, Architettura de luce a movemento (The Piper, Architecture of Light
and Movement), 1966/67, courtesy Carlo Caldini (see p 100)

Gruppo 9999 (Giorgio Birelli, Carlo Caldini, Fabrizio Fiumi, Paolo Galli),
Space Electronic, Florence, 1969, courtesy Carlo Caldini © Gruppo 9999 (see p 103)

Pietro Derossi, Altro Mondo Club, Rimini, 1967, courtesy Pietro Derossi (see p 104)

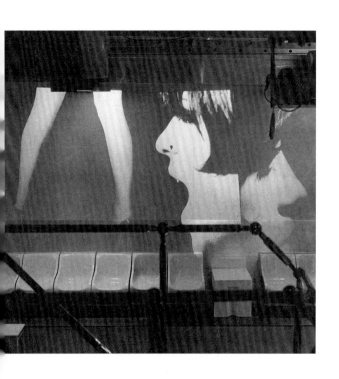

Pietro Derossi, Piper Club, Turin, 1966, courtesy Pietro Derossi (see p 105)

EXTREME CLOSEUP OF
EXPLOSION OCCURRED

EAT R+D Mirror Dome Santa Ana, courtesy Experiments in Art and Technology,
The Getty Research Institute, Los Angeles, 1969 (see p 112)

HERE

EAT Pepsi Dome Interior, Osaka, 1970
Photo: Shunk-Kender © Roy Lichtenstein Foundation (see p 114)

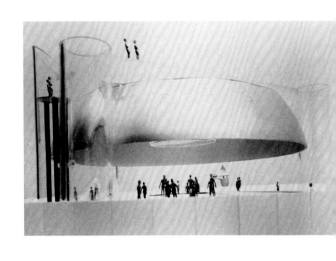

EAT Pavilion First Model, courtesy Experiments in Art and Technology,
The Getty Research Institute, Los Angeles, 1969 (see p 116)

EAT Wind Tunnel Test Kyoto University, Kazuo Murato / EAT, courtesy Experiments
in Art and Technology, The Getty Research Institute, Los Angeles, 1969 (see p 118)

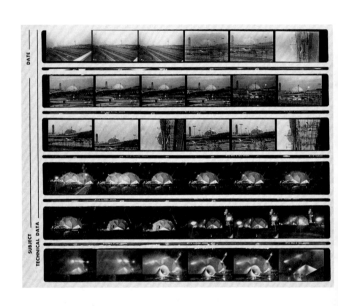

DATE

SUBJECT
TECHNICAL DATA

EAT Pepsi Dome Contact Sheet, 1969, photos: Shunk-Kender, The Getty Research
Institute, Los Angeles © Roy Lichtenstein Foundation (see p 120)

Paul Rudolph Apartment, Beekman Place, 1967
Photo: Ezra Stoller © Ezra Stoller/Esto (see p 124)

Paul Rudolph, Elman Apartment, 1971
Photo: Yukio Futagawa © GA Photographers (see p 126)

Andy Warhol at The Factory with Brillo Box
Photo: Billy Name © Billy Name (see p 127)

Carlo Mollino, untitled, c1968–73, Polaroid touched up
Courtesy Museo Casa Mollino (see p 129)

Ugo La Pietra, Altre Cose, Milan (with Paolo Rizzatto and Aldo Jacober), 1969
Courtesy Archivio Ugo La Pietra (see p 133)

View of the Festival of Britain, 1951, photo: taken from
M Banham and B Hillier (eds.) *A Tonic to the Nation: The Festival of Britain 1951*
London: Thames & Hudson, 1976, courtesy Festival of Britain Office (see p 140)

Barbara D'Arcy, *The Bloomingdale's Book of Home Decorating*, 1973
Courtesy Bloomingdale's, Inc (see p 141)

C Ray Smith, Projection of Guggenheim Museum dome in Smith Apartment, New York City, 1967, photo: Louis Reens, courtesy Richard Reens (see p 144)

Gruppo 9999, Urban Decoration (Projectual Happening), Florence, 1968
© Gruppo 9999 (see p 145)

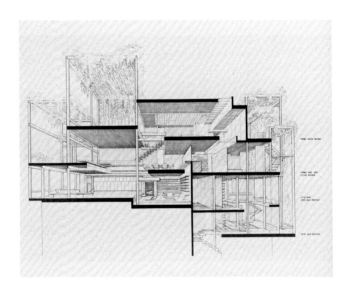

Cross-section of Paul Rudolph Apartment, 23 Beekman Place,
New York City, courtesy Library of Congress, Prints & Photographs Division
(LC-USZ62-123771) (see p 151)

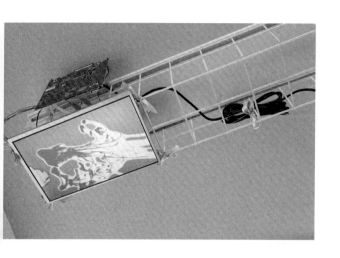

Pipilotti Rist, *Solution for Man Solution for Woman*, 2011, installation view
at Wexner Center for the Arts (in the female bathroom), Columbus, OH (2011)
Photo: Kevin Fitzsimons, courtesy the artist and Hauser & Wirth (see p 164)

Jason Payne, *Raspberry Fields*, courtesy Hirsuta (see p 175)

Arcade Fire, still from *Scenes from the Suburbs*
Photo: Eric Kayne, courtesy Arcade Fire / Eric Kayne (see p 183)

Things could certainly be worse.

MOS, *Museum of Outdoor Arts Element House*, courtesy of MOS (see p 195)

Verner Panton's Pantotower installed in an apartment for J Luber, Germany, c1968
Photo: Werner Neumeister, courtesy Neumeister Photographie
© Werner Neumeister, Munich (see p 205)

Architecture Words 13
Flash in the Pan
Sylvia Lavin

Series Editor: Brett Steele

AA Managing Editor: Thomas Weaver
AA Publications Editor: Pamela Johnston
AA Art Director: Zak Kyes
Design: Claire Lyon
Series Design: Wayne Daly, Zak Kyes
Editorial Assistants: Sarah Handelman, Clare Barrett

Set in P22 Underground Pro and Palatino

Printed in The Netherlands by Lecturis

ISBN 978-1-907896-32-3

For a catalogue of AA Publications visit
aaschool.ac.uk/publications
or email publications@aaschool.ac.uk

AA Publications
36 Bedford Square
London WCIB 3ES
T + 44 (0)20 7887 4021
F + 44 (0)20 7414 0783